LANGUAGE SHIFT AMONG THE NAVAJOS

DEBORAH HOUSE

LANGUAGE SHIFT AMONG THE NAVAJOS

IDENTITY POLITICS
AND CULTURAL CONTINUITY

THE UNIVERSITY OF ARIZONA PRESS
TUCSON

First paperbound printing 2005
The University of Arizona Press
© 2002 The Arizona Board of Regents
(∞)This book is printed on acid-free, archival-quality paper.
Manufactured in the United States of America

10 09 08 07 06 05 7 6 5 4 3 2

Library of Congress Cataloging-in-Publication Data

House, Deborah.
Language shift among the Navajos: identity politics and cultural continuity /
Deborah House.
p. cm.
Includes bibliographical references and index.
 ISBN-13: 978-0-8165-2220-0—ISBN-10: 0-8165-2220-0 (paper)
   1. Navajo language—Study and teaching—Bilingual. 2. Navajo language—Influence
   on English. 3. English language—Study and teaching—Navajo speakers. 4. Code
   switching (Linguistics). 5. Navajo Indians—Social life and customs. 6. Navajo
   philosophy. I. Title.
PM2007 .H68 2002
497'.2—dc21   2001005085

To the late Dean Jackson and his vision of what Navajo education, any education, could be—an experience rich in the benefits and blessings of harmony and balance. Thank you for your leadership, your example, and your friendship.

And to the students of Diné College, in the hope of a better world for you: better cultural understanding, more respect among all people, and an awareness and appreciation of the bonds that connect us all to each other and to the beautiful world that we are privileged to share.

CONTENTS

FIGURES

following page 55

FOREWORD

The words of Benjamin Barney, 1994:

I would say there needs to be a real strong sense of being Navajo. It's a very vague thing, so I wouldn't advise what that Navajo-ness is. I don't think there's one little picture of what this person is supposed to be. It never has been. I mean the picture of being a good adjusted [person] . . . [that] I have is from my clan family. . . . But at the same time, just a first step, I would say you need to transcend this. I had to transcend my Navajo-ness to become human, just to be at a more human level. That I as a person, living, need to have some sense of self there that I have to deal with. Not everybody does get to those. I think the Navajo formula and this little map of getting there I think is there within families, within the Navajo. It might be a slightly different map from one family to another, but you need to have that piece of a map, a sense of becoming really a person. And I really have to say that because the world is so globbed together now, we're exposed to things from all over the world as well as people of every variety and the kids have to go back to that.

And I think a good map is the original Navajo map because the original Navajo map entails having to do with Utes, having to deal with Hopis, Tewas, and all these Pueblos and all these people in the tribe that are different customs, cultures, and ways and lifestyle. That original map was a good map. And that's much more necessary now. The older [generation], my great-grandparents' age, I think, were much better at dealing with cross-cultural, cross-language, cross-religion. And they had an ease, a flowing back and forth. That particular map, I think, is much more necessary for these younger Navajos than ever before, because they will end up in Germany, they will end up in France, they will end up in Korea. They will end up in New York City, Albuquerque, Phoenix, Denver. Some of them have gone mid-west; some of them have gone east. And they are probably only seven to ten years old. And they are exposed to all this diversity at a much younger age with a very high pacedness, a pace that is quite fast. And I think they need to become aware of that a little bit earlier and not get confused. I think confusion and frustration, I often use that word over and over, a little bit more with the younger generation than I used to with my own, I have a feeling. And a sense of homeness is a bigger and more vague of a thing with the younger than with me. I think this is true all over the world. People in their forties, I think, have a sense of where they came from a little bit better, you know, than the younger kids today, which is also very true with Navajos today. And that's what I would say, "You need a map. It's a little bit more necessary. And know that you'll get confused and frustrated a lot faster at a younger age than we used to," is what I would say.

To really have a strong sense of this thing that I was talking about as a home, which means that I actually have a house and that there's a piece of land and my relatives are also there on the land and there are things around there including people, activities, and everything. I do have a political interface, a work interface, and a religion there. That's very important to me. I do have huge creative, completely free-flowing sets of people and activities surrounding me. . . . I don't quite depend on things that are from like the chapter house, from the trading post, or from Chinle, or some program from there, to tell me that . . . here's an entertaining something. . . .

I have a real strong sense also of going beyond the Navajo Reservation. . . . I end up having to reconnect with people that are professors or school-related people or even just friends in Santa Fe, in Albuquerque, Phoenix, and even further beyond—Denver, South Dakota, Wyoming. And then I often want to go back to San Francisco and have that urban reconnect there, which has a lot to do with maybe my own areas of study over the years. . . .

The thing that is very important for me is to, over the years, have people, to have relationships with people, places, and things that you're doing. But over the years, I have come to say that a lot of those are me. That first I have to have this really clear relationship with those components in me that relate to those that I am talking about, which really gets me grounded back. The life is much more fuller, happier, and more satisfied if it's rooted. And that rooting does not settle it. It's a kind of image that I started using over the years. That I do have a home, but the home is not a burden. That I have a culture, a language, but it does not stifle me. It does not bound me in. I have a religion and have a religious way, but that religious system and ways, that ceremonial system, and many of its teachings does not restrict me, does not kind of tie me up so that I'm walking a narrow religious path. These are things that I think, I really see, that makes a life much more joyous maybe.

PREFACE

My initial experience in Tsaile, Arizona, on the Navajo Reservation, was at Diné College (then Navajo Community College, or NCC) as an adjunct instructor in Northern Arizona University's 1985 summer teacher education program. I taught college courses that focused on methods and theories of language instruction, specifically English language instruction in a setting where the students' first language—Navajo—was taken for granted. At the end of that summer, I was hired by NCC as an instructor in the Foundation Studies Department, where I taught a variety of developmental English classes and held several administrative roles for almost five years. When I left, it appeared to me that English was being taken for granted and that it was the Navajo language that was beginning to be problematic. What had changed?

Perhaps nothing. Perhaps it was only that I had learned something about how language issues looked when viewed from a Navajo perspective. My initial outlook had been a pragmatic one: it was a given that the goal was for Navajo students to learn English and that their English proficiency would then enable the learning and practice of other useful and valuable things in the contemporary world. While I understood to some degree the importance of respecting and maintaining the Navajo language and culture, I still conceptualized my work as simply that of facilitating the addition of another language, some content, and some useful skills to what Navajo students brought with them to school. In those early days, the issues seemed to me pretty straightforward.

But the longer I stayed and the more I learned and the more I became acquainted with the lives and thoughts of Navajo people and the more I paid attention to what was going on around me, the more complicated and confusing my picture of Navajo and English issues became. By 1989, I felt as if I knew less, not more.

Several years later, the following questions were swirling around in my brain: Why is the focus now on maintaining a shrinking Navajo language when just a few years ago it was taken for granted as Navajos' strongest language? Why is Navajo language shift accelerating when the use of the Navajo language is no longer opposed in schools and other settings? Why is the shift accelerating when, in fact, the teaching and support of Navajo is the focus of bilingual and Navajo-as-a-second-language programs in many schools? Why is the shift accelerating when the federal government, formerly the chief opponent of Navajo language and culture, is funding language programs and curriculum and material development and has passed favorable legislation recognizing and supporting the maintenance of indigenous languages in the United States? And finally, why is the language shifting so fast when nearly every Navajo I talk to says that the Navajo language is crucial to maintaining Navajo culture and that both are part of a Navajo identity? What is going on here? What is influencing Navajo individuals, families, and other groups to speak whichever language they do? Questions such as these led me back to Tsaile in late 1993 for concentrated fieldwork—and eventually to the study reported here.

I would like to acknowledge and thank the many individuals who have helped me in countless ways, beginning with my generous friends and colleagues at Diné College: Emmanuel Agbolosoo, Wilson Aronilth, Ben Barney, Glo Brown, Ferlin Clark, Carol Dawn, Don Denetdeal, Debbie Dennison, Johnson Dennison, Martha Jackson, Rex Lee Jim, Thelma Johnson, Anthony Lee, Louise Litzin, B. Kay Manuelito, Nancy Maryboy, Marci and Jim Matlock, Dan McLaughlin, Jim McNeley, Nancy and King Mike, Mike Mitchell, Frank Morgan, Andy Natonabah, Ruth Nez, Delilah Orr, Mark Retasket, Ethel Smith, Agatha Spencer, Kay Thurston, Della Toadlena, Louise Tso, Angie Tyler, Harry and Anna Walters, Renae Walters, Karen, Paul, and Kimmy Willeto, and Sam Yessilth. Some of these people let me interview them; others were instructors in my Navajo and Indian studies classes; still others taught me through their conversations and actions. I could not have done this job without them, and I would not have loved my time in Tsaile half so much had it not been for their friendship and encouragement. *Ahe'hee*.

I am also grateful to the folks at Tsaile Elementary School, especially Polly Bitsui, Franklin Elliot, Rose Hulligan, Mary Ann Smith, and Martha White. Thanks also to the Navajo Nation Historic Preservation Office and to the Tsaile-Wheatfields Chapter.

I am indebted to the people who contributed suggestions and support in the development of my ideas: Susan Philips, Jane Hill, and Teresa McCarty, as well as Margaret Field, Donna Deyhle, and an anonymous reviewer. Those who shared other kinds of information and support were Mike and Peggy Hoffman, Allan McCartney, Gina Cantoni, M. F. Heiser, Ellen Basso, Willem de Reuse, Alice Schlegal, Irene Silentman, Roseanne Willink, Ellavina Perkins, Alyse Nuendorf, and Letty Nave.

For their funding of my research, I would like to acknowledge and thank the Phillips Fund of the American Philosophical Society and both the Graduate College and the Department of Anthropology at the University of Arizona.

I thank Yvonne Reineke, acquiring editor at the University of Arizona Press, who read my manuscript thoughtfully; her advice and encouragement contributed greatly to this book. I also want to express my appreciation to Al Schroder, assistant managing editor, Anne Keyl, design and production manager, and Jane Kepp, my copy-editor in Santa Fe, for their painstaking attention to detail. I also send a big thank-you to Karen Willeto, who took all the photographs.

Finally, I am especially grateful to my brother, John House, who has been my model and inspiration in things anthropological, and to my parents, Wayne and Sue House, who are gone now but who had the good judgment to bring me up in Alaska and Arkansas.

INTRODUCTION

Navajos without Navajo? Is the time coming when there will exist a world without the Navajo language in it? Despite the many factors that contribute to the maintenance of their language, the Navajo people are, in fact, experiencing a rapid shift from Navajo to English. For instance, Paul Platero (1992a, 1992b), a Navajo linguist, surveyed 822 students in 90 Navajo Nation preschools and learned that 17.7 percent of them were monolingual Navajo speakers, 27.9 percent were bilingual Navajo-English speakers, and 54.3 percent were monolingual speakers of English. This is despite the rich use of Navajo in the home.

How can we explain this dismaying state of affairs? I see an ideological component in this shift. Diverse and contradictory ideologies held by Navajo people about their subordination by the dominant American society have led to language (and cultural) choices and behaviors that have contributed to this alarming language situation and that will, if unchecked, result in further erosion of the language. These attitudes and opinions are organized around a powerful dichotomy that represents the Navajos and the United States as essentialized opposites, with the Navajos occupying the positive end of the spectrum and the United States the negative end. This dichotomy shapes and is shaped by a discourse that operates according to a Navajo, rather than a Euro-American, agenda. The pervasive existence and consequences of the friction between the ideological positions represented by this dichotomy are further substantiated through an analysis of the content and contexts of language use by Navajos in their contemporary institutions, especially in Navajo school settings.

THE SETTING

The fieldwork upon which this research is based was conducted in the small Navajo Nation community of Tsaile in northeastern Arizona. The Tsaile community is included in the population figure of 1,754 individuals living in the Tsaile-Wheatfields Chapter region (Navajo Nation Census 1993:60). Local businesses, facing each other across Highway 12, consist of two trading posts, one Navajo-owned and one Anglo-owned. In addition, there is a public school serving grades K–8, an Indian Health Service clinic, a nondenominational church, and the Navajo tribal college, Diné College, formerly known as Navajo Community College. In 2000, the college had a semester's enrollment of fewer than 350 students. About 95 percent of the student body was Navajo, with students coming from communities all over the Navajo Nation; the remaining 5 percent included students from other tribes, other ethnic groups in the United States, and other countries.

Most Tsaile community residents travel to Chinle, about twenty-five miles to the southwest, to shop at Bashas grocery store, to eat out at the Thunderbird Lodge, the Holiday Inn, the Canyon de Chelly Inn, the Junction Restaurant, or one of the several fast-food franchises, or to get other very basic services. More extensive shopping, services, and entertainment take residents to Gallup, New Mexico, about eighty miles south, or to another of the reservation border towns, including Farmington, New Mexico; Durango, Colorado; and Flagstaff, Arizona.

FIELDWORK AND DATA COLLECTION METHODS

In carrying out my research, I used several time-honored ethnographic methods. I was specifically interested in collecting extensive, varied, and precise data on the forms, uses, and contexts of Navajo discourse and other culturally informed Navajo behaviors. At my research site, there was no dearth of discourse about the importance for Navajo people of maintaining their distinct Navajo identity via traditional Navajo language and cultural practices. It is a topic that is aired, defined, explained, illustrated, and elaborated unceasingly. It soon became clear to me, however, that there were some glaring and inescapable discrepancies between the official and publicly sanctioned discourses of what should be—which were explicitly communicated in public nation- and identity-building events—and the unspoken and nameless ideologies that were implicit in the undiscussed yet easily visible linguistic and behavioral practices of the Navajo people as they conducted their day-to-day lives.

My data derived chiefly from four sources. The first was participant observation. Because of the diverse roles I played at Diné College throughout two periods of living and working in Tsaile, I had many and varied opportunities to carry out this research strategy. During my first stay of four and a half years in Tsaile, I worked full-time at Diné College as an instructor, as chair of an academic division, and as director of the Learning Center, which provides tutoring services to students in both

Navajo and English. In the summers during that period, I remained at the college as an adjunct professor for Northern Arizona University, teaching English as a second language, bilingual multicultural education, and English grammar classes at the undergraduate and graduate levels to students in teacher education programs. In August 1989, I left Tsaile with no idea that I would return there or to the college.

I found myself moving back to Tsaile, however, in December 1993. Beginning in January 1994 and throughout my fieldwork at Diné College and in the Tsaile community, I was again an employee of Diné College and a year-round resident. For a year and a half (1994–1995), I was the half-time director of the Student Literacy Corps, a federally funded program that placed Diné College students in the local elementary school to work with small groups of gifted students and their regular classroom teachers. During that time I also taught one English class as an adjunct instructor, served as a consultant to the fledgling Diné Teacher Education Program (an innovative bachelor of arts degree program in elementary teacher education offered by Diné College in partnership with Arizona State University), and assisted in other capacities at the college. When the grant that was funding the literacy program expired, I became a faculty member and administrator at the college. As such, I was allowed to rent one of the small modern hogans (traditional octagonal Navajo dwellings with a central wood-burning stove) made available to college employees; these are situated within easy walking distance of the college campus.

This employment and living situation gave me ample opportunities for intensive and extensive participant observation. I was able to attend many formally organized college events, both large and small, including student orientation, faculty orientation, joint meetings of Tsaile and Shiprock campus faculty, Diné College graduation, Navajo language task force meetings, curriculum committee meetings, division chairpersons' meetings, and student assemblies. I either audio-recorded these events and then transcribed and, when necessary, translated them, or else I made detailed notes while the event was under way or soon afterward. I also conducted participant observation, and sometimes just observation, at the college and in the larger community during everyday conversations, interactions, and events—at the post office, at the trading post, in the school cafeteria, in hallways, in offices, in the ladies' room, on the sidewalk, in classrooms, at my own and others' homes, in cars and trucks, at picnics and celebrations, at traditional Navajo ceremonies, and so on. For these situations, I made detailed field notes at a later time.

A second source of data was twenty structured, open-ended interviews I conducted with Navajo students, faculty, staff, and administrators from Diné College. Several of the interview questions elicited life history information. Because I conducted the interviews myself, most of the interviewees spoke in English. For the most part, they used Navajo only for routine phrases and when they were sure I would understand. Because most of these people knew me well, they gauged my Navajo language proficiency quite accurately. Occasionally, they used Navajo when there simply seemed to be no equivalent phrase in English.

The Navajos who allowed me to interview them and who provided me with the information included in this study are identified in two different ways. Most of them chose to have their real names appear in conjunction with the material they provided. These names are simply listed next to their quoted or paraphrased words. Others requested that their real names not be used, so I have given them pseudonyms. These are denoted as, for example, "Celeste Charley (pseudonym)." Collectively, these people provided much of the data I use to challenge the widespread Navajo tribal and Diné College institutional discourse, which appears to claim that there is some consensus about what it means to be Navajo today—what it means to adhere to traditional Navajo ways and teachings and what the importance of the Navajo language is in an authentic Navajo identity.

The third source of data was my class notes, handouts, and the research papers I wrote for a number of Navajo and Indian Studies courses and Navajo language courses in which I was a student, beginning in 1985 and continuing into 1996. These courses included Navajo Oral History, Navajo Oral Traditions, Foundations of Navajo Culture, Diné Educational Philosophy, Navajo Philosophy, Navajo Language I and II, and Navajo Literacy. In addition to these course materials, I include under this source heading my notes as well as the handouts I collected from a variety of pedagogical workshops, and training sessions conducted or sponsored by the college's Center for Diné Studies, the Diné Educational Philosophy Office, and the Diné Teacher Education Program. Examples of such presentations were a "Diné Language Perspectives Forum," a "Conference on Diné Philosophy: Sa'ah Naagháí Bik'eh Hózhóón Atiin 'A Pathway of Happiness,'" a "Diné Educational Philosophy Conference on Teaching and Learning with Students, Medicine Men, and Traditional Scholars," and "The Winter Stories: The Foundation of Navajo Origin."

A majority of the instructors and presenters in these classes and events were medicine men, traditional healers, herbalists, Native American Church roadmen, or elders and other recognized Navajo cultural experts. Seldom was a woman a presenter at one of these occasions; the rare woman was either a Navajo elder or a professional educator or politician. When I asked why more women did not appear in these roles, I was told that women were generally restricted from such venues for their own protection. Tonya Kayaani (pseudonym), a college employee, said,

There are a lot of things that happen in the world, things that are negative
and could hurt women. The cultural belief is that women should be protected

because of their [reproductive] role in society. For the most part, the Navajo Nation is comfortable to let women take leadership roles with areas concerning health, human services. A lot of the decision making about whether a particular woman should do this has to come from the medicine man who takes care of clans and from the oldest elders in the clans. These people have to think about the welfare of these women. Women can do more when they are past childbearing. A woman can be damaged by what she sees and what she comes in contact with; keeping women from these public roles is done more for their protection. . . . Some people may call this being chauvinist.

These classes, seminars, and training sessions were all chiefly pedagogical lectures. It is widely said that Navajos, especially the young people, are no longer being taught their culture or being given adequate opportunities to learn its teachings, values, and stories. In the past—certainly in their grandparents' generation—such knowledge was routinely transmitted as part of a family's daily and seasonal round. Songs, prayers, and other content and values were taught while people carried out household and subsistence tasks and participated in social activities in the immediate family and beyond. There were songs, prayers, and other lessons that accompanied sheepherding and gardening, weaving and basket making, bearing and tending children, greeting and interacting with others. One learned by doing and observing. In addition, many important and sacred teachings took place during ceremonies and other events that centered on the creation of the Navajo people and all that exists in the world and on the Navajo emergence into the present White or Glittering World through a succession of previous worlds. The telling of the winter stories late at night around the fire in the center of the hogan, like the playing of the shoe game, a reenactment of the gambling contest in which the animals decided the duration of night and day, was an occasion for transmitting this cultural knowledge. Yet another source of instruction about how Navajos were to behave and to live in their world was the Coyote stories—engaging tales in which Coyote loses his beautiful fur coat, or accidentally burns his pups alive, or is flattened by a rock while trying to play with lizards. They are entertaining, but they are also serious instruction about the consequences of vanity, greed, or inappropriate inquisitiveness.

Because present-day Navajo youths, as well as many of their parents, are deprived of these stories and experiences, there is a widespread belief that schools can and should attempt to provide what is missing. This is the goal behind the Navajo culture, history, and language classes at Diné College and other educational institutions of the Navajo Nation. It is the reason Diné College and other schools organize numerous seminars and cultural programs such as the ones described above, which serve tribal employees, personnel from other schools, and community members.

A fourth method of data collection was the gathering of printed materials and expired public announcements from college and other local bulletin boards. These included college memos, brochures and fliers, college newsletters, student fundraising advertisements, and the like. In addition, I collected copies of the tribal newspaper (the *Navajo Times*), the *Gallup Independent,* and local free newspapers such as the *Navajo-Hopi Observer*. These materials revealed relatively unselfconscious ideas about appropriate uses of language—Navajo and English—and of images and discourses reflecting language and cultural ideology among the Navajo people. I found it interesting, for instance, that fund-raising on the Navajo Reservation almost always involved the selling or raffling of Navajo cultural items—Navajo tacos (a round of fry bread topped with chili beans, shredded lettuce, chopped onions, and chopped tomatoes—served with salsa and a can of pop), silver and turquoise jewelry, a Pendleton blanket, perhaps a sheep—or admission to a traditional Navajo or other Indian event, such as a traditional song and dance performance, a Native American music concert, a rodeo, or a powwow.

LANGUAGE SHIFT

Before proceeding with my own analysis of the ideological component in Navajo language shift, I should mention several aspects of the general topic of language shift that are particularly relevant to this study. Two fields have provided the bulk of the literature: linguistics and education. Linguists have made valuable contributions to the study of Navajo language shift by describing the current health and future outlook of languages experiencing shift (see, for example, Brandt 1988; Hale et al. 1992; Krauss 1996; Platero 1992a, 1992b; Slate 1993a, 1993b; Veltman 1983; Young 1983). Ofelia Zepeda and Jane Hill (1991) and Joshua Fishman (1991) have contributed to this literature by summarizing data on specific languages and generalizing about the factors that favor language shift and about policies and practices that have proved valuable in halting or reversing it. This breadth in knowledge of the topic allows for the generation of typologies that assist others in assessing for themselves the health of, and prognosis for, targeted languages.

The field of Native American education is another source of valuable data, as well as insights and advice, about Native American language use and disuse. Two Navajo Nation schools have won the interest and respect of those working toward indigenous language instruction and maintenance—Rough Rock (Benally and McCarty 1990; McCarty 1989; McCarty et al. 1991) and Rock Point (Bingham and Bingham 1982; Holm 1971, 1993; Holm and Holm 1990; McLaughlin 1990, 1992;

Robert Roessel 1979; Ruth Roessel 1971; Rosier and Holm 1980; Spolsky 1975a, 1975b). The extensive literature on these two schools details the characteristics they share that have been key to their exceptional success. Both schools have been community owned and operated for a long time, and both implemented innovative bilingual-bicultural programs that focused on maintenance rather than transitional goals. Both benefited from determined and charismatic leadership and were committed to becoming distinctive Navajo schools serving Navajo-defined needs.

Other studies providing valuable information about Navajo-related language issues include Donna Deyhle's long-term work in schools on the Arizona-Utah border (Deyhle 1983, 1986a, 1986b, 1995), Vera John's (1972) discussion of the effects of Navajo learning styles on students' experiences in school, and Evangeline Parsons-Yazzie's (1995; Yazzie 1995) dissertation research in the Hardrock community in Arizona, which gives us Navajo-speaking parents' explanations for Navajo language shift among their children, followed by their recommendations about measures that could be taken to reverse the situation.

This literature hammers home the point that language shift is a complex phenomenon with multiple, interacting causes; problems in one social or political area are exacerbated by those in another. Likewise, these authors make it abundantly clear that there are no simple prescriptions for language loss, and no effortless transformations of the social and political environments in which shift occurs.

NAVAJO CULTURAL AND LINGUISTIC IDEOLOGY

Gary Witherspoon, a long-time student of Navajo culture, once wrote: "The behavior and institutions of another people must be viewed, at least initially, against the backdrop of their view of the world or their ideological frame of reference. Their conception of the nature of reality, its operation and constitution, shapes their value orientations, behavioral codes, and classificatory structures" (1977:4). The connection between behavior and institutions, on the one hand, and worldview and ideology, on the other, is an important thing to emphasize at the beginning of a discussion of Navajo ideology; it is a point that others have made before. Such an ideology is a statement of how Navajos conceptualize their relationships with other entities in their universe in terms of who can act on whom, who can compel or control whom. This is a basic statement of a hierarchical relationship, and it is human nature to have a sense of where one fits in such a hierarchy.

In order to begin to see the ideologies connected with Navajo language, one must back up and look at the broader context within which language ideology operates. Its roots lie in Navajos' understandings of their history and their political relations with the dominant United States society. In the eyes of many Navajos, the defining moment of their nearly five hundred years of contact and conflict with non-Navajos was their capture, removal from their homeland within the four sacred mountains, and incarceration in New Mexico in 1863 after the bitter journey known as the Long Walk. That milestone and the constellation of circumstances associated with it have established among many contemporary Navajo people a world-view that pits Navajos (conceived of as a single, homogeneous, racial, ethnic, national, linguistic, religious, and political entity—usually characterized simply as "Navajo culture") against an equally undifferentiated and essentialized West (routinely thought of as American whites but often expanded to include almost all non-Indians). The latter group is variously labeled "the West," Anglos, *bilagáana*s ("white men" or "Anglos"), Western society, Western civilization, mainstream society, the dominant society, and "the white man." And English, as a rule, is the language that Navajos associate with this mass of people.

Language issues (specifically the contest between Navajo and English) cannot be understood or discussed productively outside of that pervasive conceptualization. Knowing that these ideologies act upon and are acted upon by specific aspects of the "cultural" and linguistic lives of Navajos, I view language itself (its literal content and its actual use—oral and written), as well as nonlanguage actions and displays, as a location in which to recognize these ideologies. Nonlanguage sites may involve both everyday and ceremonial behavior, including actions organized around family, spiritual, educational, professional, and social events; around art, craft, music, and architectural productions; and around clothing, hairdressing, and ornamentation of person and space.

One can distinguish between occasions or sites in which ideology is explicit and others in which it is implicit. An example of an explicit ideological statement is this one by Renae Walters, a former Diné College student: "I just feel that, you know, the United States government tried to take [the Navajo language] away from us. They almost succeeded, you know; you see people who are ashamed of who they are and I'd like to think it's part of the United States' fault that we're this way, we're in this situation today. It's because of them; they abused us; they put our ancestors, they made them walk on the Long Walk. They made, you know, the older people not want to . . . talk Navajo" (April 4, 1995).

This statement clearly indexes the dominant-subordinate relationship between the United States and the Navajos and represents the former as holding the power. A more implicit ideological statement is this one, by the same student: "I looked at my life and I thought, 'I don't want to live like this. I don't want to be this way forever because I don't want to stand on the welfare line for the rest of my life and have someone spoon-feed me and give me money, work for me. . . . I don't want to stand on the welfare line and, you know, just be nothing for the rest of my life, and I don't want to have a drinking problem. I don't want to be a drunk in Gallup or Page or whatever, you know.' So somehow I knew I had to change, so I tried to do a lot of things to change myself in a lot of ways." Here, she again refers to the relationship between the United States and the Navajo people. By calling up a common negative stereotype that outsiders (as well as some Navajos) have of what it means to be Navajo, she alludes to a relationship in which the United States government is in control. This time, however, she acknowledges that resistance and action are possible.

Relations of dominance and subordination are also important in language issues. In many cases, the use of one language in addition to or in place of another is ideologically inspired—having everything to do with the political motivations and consequences of bringing two or more language-using peoples together. Navajo language ideology, then, is connected to Navajo ideology in general. Depending on the context, we could discuss Navajo ideologies about "traditional" Navajo culture, about Navajo culture (with adoptions and incorporations from other cultures), or about contemporary Navajo culture (which exists in conjunction with Western hegemony). A discussion of the language ideologies held by Navajos might include the ideologies they have or have had about Navajo language (as if Navajo were the only language used by Navajos), about Navajo language in contemporary society (in which Navajos also use and are affected by English), about the use of English and Navajo as equal languages, and about the possibility that English might one day be the only language of the Navajos.

Language ideologies in a Navajo context truly cannot usefully be separated from ideologies concerning thought, from action or other behavior, from knowledge, or from the material world. The discourse and literature about the Navajos, both by themselves and by others, make this abundantly clear. In discusssions of Navajo worldview, Navajo spirituality, Navajo lifestyle, Navajo education, Navajo politics, and Navajo art, the interconnectedness of the various elements is foregrounded again and again.

Another, equally crucial body of literature that adds to our understanding of ideologies associated with the Navajo language comes from studies of the role of the language in Navajo cosmic and spiritual beliefs and the functions and meanings of Navajo ceremonialism. The two scholars who have provided the most compelling insights into this realm are Gladys Reichard and Gary Witherspoon. Their work is of exceptional interest and utility for similar reasons. Both lived and worked among Navajo people for many years, participating fully and actively in the everyday lives of the people. Their unromantic respect and admiration shines through their words. In setting forth their analyses and conclusions, both provide a wealth of precise and illuminating linguistic and contextual detail to substantiate their claims.

Among Reichard's considerable writings on the Navajos, *Navaho Religion* (1950) and *Prayer: The Compulsive Word* (1944) are of particular interest to those who wish to know more about the ideologies held by Navajo people (as a generalized group) about the nature and functions of their language. Reichard more than convinces the reader that language and thought often function as a pair with active agency in the Navajo world—both in the general sense that the universe was brought into being by language and in the sense that language in the form of specific constructions (such as words, word formulas, prayers, and songs) has a power that can be directed to positive or negative ends. She writes extensively about the compulsive and irresistible power of prayer and song—within ceremonies and outside them—to secure the assistance of the Holy People for human purposes. But with the power that is inherent in language comes danger, so that use of language requires respect, caution, and even avoidance for those unable, unwilling, or unprepared to assume such risks. If language is the risk, however, it is also the source of protection.

These insights into Navajos' own beliefs about their language are directly applicable to an informed analysis of contemporary Navajo language practices. Three examples of such practices are the use of silence in situations of uncertainty, the importance of a facility for Navajo language and Navajo-style oratory for a Navajo political candidate, and the prevalence of Navajo men in public leadership and therefore in speaking roles.

Influenced by the work of Reichard, whom he greatly admires, Witherspoon, too, has given considerable attention to the potency of language in the Navajo world. In numerous articles (1971, 1974, 1975, 1983) and in his book *Language and Art in the Navajo Universe* (1977), he meticulously describes and explains his understanding of the Navajo worldview and how it is reflected in Navajo conceptions of reality and causality and in their everyday thought and behavior. He concludes that "the primary metaphysical assumption on which the Navajo view of the world is built is the opposition between active and static phenomena or active and static phases of phenomena." He explains that this dualism provides a metaphysical framework for Navajo conceptualizations of the relationships and interactions among thought, speech, knowledge, and elements in the material world. A chief characteristic of such relationships is a hierarchy that expresses who or what can act on or assert control over another; this is the concept underlying the compulsive power of thought and language in ritual contexts. Ultimately, he says, "these concepts of reality are translated into everyday behavioral patterns and value orientations" (1977:179).

While accepting these insights into the timeless Navajo universe, I found myself wanting to know more about how this worldview has been affected by the present-day bilingualism and biculturalism of the majority of Navajo people. I hope the subsequent chapters in this book show that new materials and elements, applications, and examples situated in the modern world are relevant.

THE DANGERS
OF ESSENTIALIZING

An additional important point is that much of the work by scholars of Navajo life and material culture can be somewhat misleading. As one reads one generalizing scheme after another (Farella 1984; McNeley 1981; Witherspoon 1977), it becomes clear that although there are enormous areas of overlap and agreement, there are also differences in emphasis and in the resulting conceptual "maps" or "images" of who the Navajos are. What each writer about Navajo culture, art, language, or ceremonials knows and represents is necessarily partial. There is no longer, and perhaps there never truly was, a homogeneous entity known as "the Navajo." Perhaps there was more justification for this usage in the past; perhaps there was greater uniformity and consensus in the period before Spanish contact, or before American contact, or in 1868, or at some other time in the past. Perhaps there indeed was a time when a statement about "the Navajos" was likely to characterize a majority of the Navajo people.

If so, however, that time has passed. This is a hard thing to say and a hard thing to hear. Yet the essentializing discourse that represents the past as present is alive and well. It is fed by Anglos and Navajos alike, whether they are politicians, educators, artists, or anthropologists. It is difficult to break old habits. Furthermore, there are many reasons for continuing this monolithic usage, particularly because it has stabilized around such positive images and values. It allows political negotiations to proceed with somewhat greater ease if both sides (Navajo and Anglo) can say, "The Navajos are *X;* the Navajos need *Y.*" It allows commercial products to be marketed with greater success if both sides can say, "This is a traditional Navajo design; this was made by a traditional Navajo artist; this is based on traditional Navajo stories." It also allows individuals to identify with a whole that is more beautiful, more spiritual, more peaceful, and stronger than any mere individual could possibly be. It oversimplifies the world into "us" and "them" and makes interactions simple.

Despite the many positive aspects of such essentializing (and I do not deny that these exist), there are also dangers. I could point out that the necessity of recognizing that every positive thing also has a negative aspect is a time-honored "traditional" Navajo teaching. I believe that for Navajos (individuals or the Navajo

Nation as a whole) to represent "the Navajo" of the present to *themselves* as a single uniform entity characterized by the unvarying descriptions that have been used for the past hundred years or so is dangerous, because it prevents them from recognizing the fact or the possible consequences of steady language and culture erosion. Complacent people are unlikely to take action against such a threat. I will say much more about this later.

Saying that "Navajos have no word for religion," which was no doubt true for monolingual speakers of Navajo at some point in the past, is *not* true of Navajos today. Most Navajos today are bilingual; many are monolingual English speakers. These people do have a word for religion; it is "religion." The word and the concept were introduced more than a hundred years ago, and most Navajos today have never *not* had the word or the concept. Many of these people, in fact, actively practice a genuine Western-style religion: they are Baptists, Methodists, Catholics, Lutherans, or Mormons, despite the fact that such denominations were forcibly imposed on many Navajos in the past. Still others participate in an organized religion—the Native American Church—that contains significant, undeniably Christian religious elements.

It is also said and written repeatedly that the base of Navajo culture is intact—that the strength of "the Navajo" is their ability to adopt and incorporate elements from other cultures while retaining their cultural core, which is made up of a value system that emphasizes the interrelatedness of all things, a family system organized around clan affiliations, and a language that represents and assures a continued Navajo world and worldview.

According to what I have heard hundreds of Navajos say, there is a sense that for many Navajos the "traditional" Navajo cultural core *is not intact*. It is crumbling; it is in danger of changing beyond what is safe and necessary for the Navajos as a people. For many, the Navajo language base is *not* everywhere, and it is not intact in every speaker of Navajo. The language is changing in structure from generation to generation; it is being taught to fewer young people; it is being spoken by fewer of the people who could speak it if they chose to. A growing proportion of Navajos do not use it to address the Holy People in ceremonies and prayers and songs; not all Navajos use it to bring the world back into harmony and balance. This is not what many of us—Navajos and Anglos alike—want to hear. We want to believe there is somewhere, someplace, where things are as they should be; we want to believe that in this sane, beautiful place that exists somewhere, there is hope and an example for all of us who look forward to a benign future where the problems that surround and even emanate from the Anglo world will not exist. We want this badly.

My point is that unless we all acknowledge the problems that surround us and look them in the face and call them by name, we cannot begin to solve them. My point is that unless Navajos—individually and as a nation—acknowledge the undeniable attrition of their language and their culture base, and also acknowledge that many of the remedial efforts that have been attempted are not working, they cannot begin to reverse the process.

My personal conviction is that this is an important thing. I believe that the world—the Navajo world and my own world—would be a better place with Navajo culture and Navajo language alive and strong, being transmitted from generation to generation indefinitely. But I also believe it is not my call—not my decision whether this should be done, not my decision how to do it, not my business to judge which degree or which version or which aspect of Navajo-ness is the goal. These decisions and plans must be made and implemented by Navajos themselves.

Navajos are faced with the dilemma of how to create an authentic yet viable Navajo identity in an irreversibly modern world. I suggest a return to the central Navajo philosophical paradigm—Sa'ąh Naagháí Bik'eh Hózhóón—which historically and in the present has the potential to provide the key to maintaining personal as well as group balance and harmony in a dynamic and evolving world. It is said that this process was designed by the Holy People to assure "long life happiness." I suggest that it might also play a role in reversing Navajo language shift.

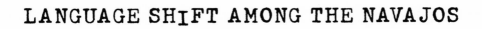

LANGUAGE SHIFT AMONG THE NAVAJOS

HEGEMONY, IDEOLOGY, AND "CULTURE"

ONE

A way of life, a way of thinking about themselves, ended for the Navajos with their military conquest by Americans. Writing about another time and other nations, Edward Said (1993:147) described a "great symbolic event by which the two sides achieved their full and conscious opposition to each other." For the Navajos and their later relationship with the United States, their Long Walk and subsequent four-year incarceration at Hwééldi, or Fort Sumner, was, and continues to be, just such an event. The physical and psychological damage this experience inflicted upon the Navajo people can hardly be overstated.

Harrowing accounts of this period come from an Indian Claims Commission meeting held on January 16 and 17, 1951. Dougal Chee Bekis, who was born west of Fort Wingate a few days after his family returned home from New Mexico, described the ordeal that women, children, and even old people had experienced, as it had been recounted to him. Bill Acrey (1979:51) described this testimony. Bekis said that the Navajos "had to keep up the same pace as the march was making. Some were even on crutches; when they could not go any more, they [the soldiers] disposed of them. They did not know where they were going or why they were going. . . . They were terribly frightened to the extent that they were moaning and so on. They were not riding horses, they were talking to themselves saying, 'My country, my land. I will probably die somewhere between here and the destination.' They were terribly frightened." Though not all Navajos could be caught and taken to Fort Sumner, by December 1864 there were 8,354 Navajos living in the camp.

Peter Iverson (1981:9–10) described the Navajos' reaction to this incarceration:

> They remember not only the Long Walk but the years at Hwééldi with great
> bitterness, and there was much to be bitter about: the forced march itself, the

barren surroundings in which they found themselves, the very fact of impris-
onment, and the homesickness, illness, hunger, and discomfort that charac-
terized life at the Bosque. At the same time, they remember the ability of their
forefathers to persevere, and they emphasize the role of traditional Navajo
religion in allowing them to return to their homeland. One man recalled
a special ceremony that immediately preceded the announcement that the
Navajos could return home; one woman stated that Navajo singers performed
several ceremonies "to find out whether they would be released," and "they
could see their release in the near future."

Eventually, the Navajos were allowed to return to their beloved, but much reduced, homeland under the terms of the Treaty of 1868 with the United States. A number of the terms of this treaty were initially perceived to be onerous and intrusive; they would later be cited, however, as spelling out rights and benefits that the Navajo people insist upon as part of their "special" or sovereign status. These rights include, but are not limited to, designated reservation land, formal Western schooling, and social services.

The political relationship between Navajos and Americans was thus established. During the conflict and military engagements that brought the Navajos to their imprisonment, the American government exerted outright domination of the Navajo people. This was followed by a period of colonization and control that gradually yielded to a debatable degree of hegemonic incorporation. This hegemony on the part of the United States has been asserted over the years through a number of state institutions (governmental structures, schools, health and social services) as well as civil institutions (churches and businesses).

AMERICAN INCORPORATION OF THE NAVAJOS

Although the American government clearly dominated the Navajos, its actual control over Navajo life was ameliorated by the reservation's effective isolation. Because of the Navajos' physical distance from and lack of communication with the outside world, American cultural influences—in those days manifested chiefly through traders, missionaries, and teachers who brought a rudimentary Western education—were only slowly and gradually felt. Certainly, many such Americans had little interest in preserving Navajo language and culture, but they were limited in their negative impact on the Navajos because they tended to focus only on whichever aspect of Navajo life came immediately under their purview. The missionaries were concerned primarily with Navajo souls (and labor); they aimed at reforming the religious and spiritual side of Navajo life.

Traders were interested in their own economic profit and perhaps, to the extent that it benefited them, in facilitating the Navajos' transition to a cash economy and a "modern" lifestyle reliant on Western commercial products. The educators were chiefly interested in Navajo students' language and academic performance. At times, as in the case of boarding schools, the target areas came together, and students were expected to concentrate on the English language, Western academic topics, a new religion, and work experience (via vocational programs and "outing" experiences in Anglo families) all at once. The effects of these various institutions on Navajo culture were slight in the beginning but gained in momentum and force with time.

By the 1920s, American impact on the Navajos was beginning to be quite strong. Valuable mineral and oil resources had been discovered on Navajo land, and outsiders thirsted to exploit them. Certain Navajo leaders saw benefits to their people in this direction as well. Americans' growing need to communicate and negotiate with Navajos and to establish administrative bases on the reservation brought the Navajo people increasingly into the American sphere of influence and responsibility. Programs for administration and for improving transportation, health, and education services were implemented. Though positive in many ways for Navajos, these programs also exerted tremendous pressure on Navajo culture, introducing an unending array of new practices, material goods, and foreign values.

In 1928, Lewis Meriam's *The Problem of Indian Administration,* a comprehensive survey that spelled out the economic and social conditions of Indian life under the federal government, was published. This report makes interesting reading. It was based on an extensive survey of the living situations of American Indians at the time, and it uncovered extreme shortcomings in all aspects of government services to Indian people. It reported that schools, especially federal boarding schools, were crowded and that students were underfed and overworked as they performed strenuous "chores" (often defined as "vocational training") in order to keep the schools in operation. In response to these and other abuses, the report outlined the fundamental task of the Indian Service (later to become the Bureau of Indian Affairs, or BIA). It was that the Indian Service "be recognized as primarily educational, in the broadest sense of that word, and that it be made an efficient educational agency, devoting its main energies to the social and economic advancement of the Indians, so that they may be absorbed into the prevailing civilization or be fitted to live in the presence of that civilization at least in accordance with a minimum standard of health and decency" (Szasz 1974:64–65).

Outlining the services and the education that should be provided for Indian adults and children, the Meriam report also specified that the rights of Indians must be respected—that they should not be forced into a lifestyle that was abhorrent to them. Rather, they should be aided in maintaining their own culture and "mode of life" in recognition of the damage done to the previous economic basis of their culture. Furthermore, Indians should be educated to assume control over their own affairs (Prucha 1975:219–221).

In response to the charges of the Meriam report, the Indian Service embarked on a New Deal for Indian education. Inspired by the progressive educational philosophy of John Dewey and by the humanistic anthropology of the time, Indian Service officials partook of an idealistic and radical time in Native American education. When John Collier became commissioner of Indian affairs in 1933, he brought a new philosophy to the conduct of that office. The central tenet of his policy was a steadfast rejection of former efforts to assimilate Indians into the dominant culture. He favored a philosophy of cultural pluralism that allowed and even encouraged Indians to retain their ethnic and cultural identity (Parman 1972:xi).

This philosophical stance resulted in a number of drastic policy changes. Community day schools became the favored school system, and as many boarding schools as possible were closed. On the Navajo Reservation, four experimental "hogan schools" were constructed—at Mariano Lake, Cove, Navajo Mountain, and Shonto. Significant changes were made in the curricula of reservation schools, with a trend toward culturally relevant materials. Bilingual programs were preferred when trained teachers were available to carry them out. Navajos were encouraged to view the day schools as centers for community activities. For the first time, some parents became comfortable with the idea of sending their children to school.

Although day schools were preferred, some boarding schools were still needed to serve students who simply lived too far away to be transported back and forth to day schools. These boarding schools, however, were an improvement over the earlier ones. The strict military routines of the 1920s were considerably modified, and administrators tried harder to make student labor more relevant to future reservation jobs.

To some extent, Bureau of Indian Affairs educators recognized the importance of traditional culture to their Native American clientele. In order to present this culture as subject matter in the schools, they broke the whole of culture up into discrete components—history, customs and traditions, religion, art, language, philosophy, social structure and regulations, and value system. Only three of these components, however—history, art, and language—found their way into the curricula (Szasz 1974:50–59, 66–67).

Although those at the top administrative levels attempted to further develop bilingual and bicultural programs, their efforts were met with extreme disfavor by many politicians, bureaucrats, and even some Navajos. People who saw monolingual English as essential to assimilation and to personal and economic success felt that such programs at best postponed the inevitable and at worst seriously handicapped the Navajo child. Those who did not understand the goals of a bilingual maintenance program saw it as an inferior program that would not give students the English language or cultural competence necessary to compete in the Anglo world. The same criticisms are heard today.

Strong opponents of Collier's school programs were Jacob Morgan and his followers. These Navajos had attended boarding schools at their most rigid and militaristic. Learning at such schools was a serious and often difficult business, and many of those who had been educated at these institutions could not understand the concept of "learning by playing" in the modern, progressive day schools. Even more than most Navajos, the Morgan faction saw Western education as the pathway to individual and tribal economic advancement; its members demanded that the school curriculum stress English and other subjects associated with Anglo culture (Parman 1972).

During Collier's administration, Robert W. Young, an Anglo graduate student in linguistics, and William Morgan, a young Navajo, developed a simplified orthography of the Navajo language that used only existing English letters and a minimum of supplemental diacritics to indicate nasal sounds and tonal qualities. The first primer resulting from their efforts was published in 1940. Its stories were in both Navajo and English and depicted reservation life. All of these stories were illustrated by Navajo artists (Young 1993).

The availability of written Navajo made it possible to write instructional materials that would add relevance to students' education. Also, it was believed that teaching beginning students to read Navajo would materially shorten the time they required to learn English. For the tribe as a whole, written Navajo would reduce the misunderstandings and confusion that often arose because Navajos and Anglo government officials could not communicate. It would now be possible to post written information at schools and trading posts and to circulate it in the tribal newspaper (Holm 1971).

Until World War II, the vast reservation had existed out of the mainstream of the dominant Anglo culture. The traditional economy of sheepherding, farming, silversmithing, and weaving had been more or less adequate for Navajo needs. The Navajo language had been more than adequate for those who were monolingual. On the reservation and in the border towns, one could conduct almost any sort of business or social activity with only the Navajo language (Spolsky 1975a:3).

During the World War II era, little government attention or resources were spared for the Navajos. However, the experiences of Navajo people in the military (including travel, not only off reservation but to other countries) and work in war industries and other wage jobs put an end to the Navajos' physical and cultural isolation and led them to actively request federal involvement in their affairs. In the mid-1940s, the Navajo Tribal Council expressed its new attitude toward federal education when it sent a delegation to Washington, D.C., demanding the fulfillment of the education article that had been negotiated in the Treaty of 1868 (Szasz 1974:115; Thompson 1975:79).

About this time, the Bureau of Indian Affairs commissioned George Sanchez of the University of Texas to study the education situation on the Navajo Reservation. The results were shocking enough to require no prompting to action by the federal government. Sanchez reported that two-thirds of the population at the time had no schooling, and the median time in school completed by Navajos was less than one year. He went on to say that the old boarding-school facilities had outlived their usefulness, and he recommended spending an estimated $90 million on a controversial, reservation-wide system of community schools (Sanchez 1948; see also Robert Roessel 1979:15–16; Thompson 1975:78).

By 1946, only about six thousand of an estimated twenty-four thousand Navajo children between the ages of six and eighteen were in school (Coombs 1962). The government's solution, the Special Navajo Education Program, was the opposite of what Sanchez envisioned. It would take the older Navajo student (twelve to eighteen years of age) and provide a five-year crash course in general knowledge of Anglo culture, including English, and in vocational training. The first three years were to be devoted to learning English and other academic subjects. At the end of this time, the student was to choose a vocational field and devote the remaining two years to training for it. The last portion of this training period was to be spent in a work situation in an Anglo home, where the student's induction into the Anglo world would be completed (Thompson 1975:89).

Because there were no appropriate facilities near the reservation, the first site of this program was the vacant buildings of the Sherman Institute in Riverside, California. Two hundred students were recruited for the first session in the school year of 1946–1947, and later, room was made for ninety more. Thousands of Navajo students were educated at the Sherman Institute, and ten other such programs had come into being by 1956 (Thompson 1975:105). By 1959, this program had served more than fifty thousand students (Coombs 1962).

Martha Jackson, a Navajo language instructor at Diné College, described at length her experiences with these education and employment opportunities. Note the "outing" program in which she learned domestic job skills, as well as the Old Testament verses she was made to learn while working "like a slave" for her employer:

But the time I really started my schooling was, I must have been about thirteen, fourteen when I was sent to Sherman Institute where I went to school and got my vocational training. I didn't know why I was down there.... See, when I went to Sherman Institute, I was staying with some people, and I cleaned their house and stayed with them in their home.... And I was there five years. And she really helped me to speak English. She tried to get me into the night school. I just couldn't; I guess I really wasn't ready. And I didn't really know what I was doing anyway. So she really used to get mad at me, too. She got frustrated and I'd get frustrated and I threw the Bible back at her because my Bible was my textbook then. That was my textbook and I learned to read and write from that. And then, after we'd cool off, we would go back to the study room, you know, then she would try to talk to me. All these things that she told me, Old Testament, you know. Back then, I didn't know what I was saying, but she made me memorize, "Let the word of my mouth and the meditation of my heart. Let me be acceptable in thy sight, oh Lord."

And five years is a long time to stay with this lady.... So they had a home in Long Island and I used to travel with them or I could get on the plane and I could travel by myself.... I spoke enough English to get along. If I was hungry, I would get food. If I was lost, I would find my way, you know. She kind of introduced me to the world. And then she dropped me like a hot potato, you know.

And my memory [because of the ability to memorize scriptures] was such that later on I was able to get a job at the Grand Canyon at the Bright Angel Lodge. I did a really good job, too, because of the Jewish lady. I could scrub, you know, I scrubbed the toilet with a toothbrush, too, you know. I was very very very fortunate that way. Although it may have been mean, you might call it mean, she made a slave out of me. But that got me [a lot of skills I could use]. And that got me a job at the Grand Canyon. I became a maid. Pretty soon I was elevated to become a maid over the whole bunch. And then, from there I went into the cafeteria where I cleaned table. I did it so well that they even wanted me to be a waitress. And then they promoted me, that's when my memory that used to memorize verses, I didn't really know how to read and write and I had to do my addition and everything, so if a whole bunch of people came in, I would just take it in my memory. Like they would order and I knew just exactly where they went. See, if you can't do it one way, there's no such thing as not knowing how to do it. You can do it, that's what I tell my students now. "Use your strong point. Use your strength to get over your weakness. Instead of improving your weakness, you know, kick that out and work on your strong points." That's what I did.... After that, after they settled and were eating, I *went behind the door and took a menu, one at a time, you know. Pretty soon I memorized the whole menu, and the prices. That's how I got into reading and writing. And my turning point. And when I became a waitress, well, then I started reading* True Confession. *And believe me that's the only thing that I understood as far as reading. You know. That's the only thing I understood.*

[Her husband got cancer; she became a Christian.] It was just like his days were numbered. And I started thinking, "What am I going to do?" I knew that I would be all right and would find myself with my kids. The only thing that I knew how to do was wait tables. I did it for eleven years. . . . And I thought that was not nice. So I went and told my uncle, you know, what was happening. And he told me, he says, "Go back to school. Go back to school and get an education." . . . He always pushed me. And I didn't know why. He just said that when my mom was dying, he promised that he would take care of me. My dad said, "Don't let this child ever just waste time." He said, "Put her to school. Let her get, you know, get ahead in the world that way, so she'll be taken care of." That's what my dad said. . . . It was my uncle that pushed me. And he said, "This is why you need to go." And then so I thought, "Where can I go? What can I do?"

So I went to Tuba City. That was my first trip, from the Grand Canyon to Tuba City. I went to the Bureau of Indian Affairs and then the Indian Affairs Office. I said, "I want to go back to school. Here's the situation. We have bills like, you know, stacked high. We owe our soul to Flagstaff Hospital." I said, "My husband has cancer. He's getting treated now. But, I think it would never be a time for this. And I have five kids; I only have five kids." I said, "I want to go back to school." So they said, "First of all, we can't send you all by yourself." So I went home and told Gene [her husband] we needed to go. He said, "No, you are not going to." So I went back to the office and said, "He doesn't want to go," and they said, "Well, you either get a legal separation or divorce him." They couldn't sent me alone. So I went home. I told him. I got mad. I did everything—kicked and screamed and finally he drove all the way to, we were relocated in Los Alamos, New Mexico. . . . And they paid for our bills. And they paid that and all his medical bills, everything. We owed nothing. And they paid for our schooling and then, plus we were getting twenty-eight dollars each week, you know. (September 26, 1993)

In *Doorway toward the Light: The Story of the Special Navajo Education Program,* L. Madison Coombs (1962) described this type of five-year program (as it was known) and its results in glowing terms. He strongly favored assimilation of the

Navajos into the United States working class, and he saw this special program as molding Navajo youths to take their places in menial, off-reservation jobs. Other programs, which targeted older students and returning veterans, were offered under the G.I. Bill of Rights and the Vocational Rehabilitation Bill. Both provided academic and vocational training (Szasz 1974:119).

In 1950, the Navajo-Hopi Long Range Rehabilitation Act was passed. In recognition of the desperate need for basic services on the Navajo Reservation, the act created a comprehensive development program that would provide money over a ten-year span for water and other natural resources, health concerns, communications, housing and credit, resettlement of Navajos off reservation, and education (Thompson 1975:119).

In the 1950s, the Navajo Emergency Education Program was put into effect to give as many Navajo children as possible the opportunity to go to school. It used a number of cheap and quick approaches: trailer schools, enlarged boarding schools, public schools on the reservation, dormitories for public school students in border towns, and continuation of the Special Navajo Education Program. Despite the makeshift nature of some of these arrangements, they were successful in raising the percentage of Navajo children in school to 88.6 by 1958 (Robert Roessel 1979:22–38; Szasz 1974:125–126).

Many Navajo children were going to public schools financed through the 1934 Johnson-O'Malley Act (amended in 1936). This act authorized the Department of the Interior to contract with public school districts to provide educational services for Indians (Thompson 1975:142). Other schools serving the Navajos were church schools. One was St. Michael's Catholic Mission School, financed by Mother Drexel, founder of the Order of Sisters of the Blessed Sacrament. Others were the Navajo Methodist Mission School at Farmington, New Mexico, which had opened in 1899 for elementary school children, and the Ganado Mission School, opened by the Presbyterians at Ganado, Arizona, in 1902. Still other missionary groups—Seventh-day Adventists, Church of the Brethren, Mennonites, Lutherans, Episcopalians, and more—established church-affiliated schools (Thompson 1975:146). Though other governmental efforts and actions over the years have supported and advocated assimilation (and cultural replacement), they have been less encompassing and drastic than many of these school programs.

In the second half of the 1960s, the Navajos, like other tribes, were caught up in the widening ripples of the civil rights movement. At a time when African Americans were forging their way into the political and social mainstream of the country, Native Americans, too, were recognizing that there were many benefits to be gained by flexing their political muscles. The outgrowth of the associated political, social, and economic trends was that American Indians began to attract widespread attention and approbation—resulting in the stirring among them of self-determination and an accompanying economic boom.

Among the Navajos, this trend was particularly evident in the establishment of the Office of Navajo Economic Opportunity (ONEO) and the self-determination movement in education. Using money available through the Office of Economic Opportunity in Washington, D.C., ONEO became a powerful and influential force in supporting Navajo initiatives. By the end of 1965, this Navajo-run, locally centered program had established an extensive preschool program, a small business development center, a Neighborhood Youth Corps summer program, a "reservation-wide" recreation and physical fitness program, and a local community development program. In the years ahead, ONEO continued to expand and to benefit "almost everyone living in the Navajo Nation" (Iverson 1981:90).

For almost two decades, the Navajos rode this wave of comparative prosperity—with income from mineral leases and a shower of financial support from federal programs as well as from private foundations and other sources. The current era of social and economic conservatism has come as a rude and unwelcome shock to the Navajo people. Federal and private sources of funding are drying up, and the tribe has few means to replace them.

NAVAJO GOALS: AUTHENTIC IDENTITY AND AUTONOMY

It was the era of self-determination that saw the rise of a powerful and pervasive discourse both to represent and to construct a distinctive Navajo-ness. The supreme challenge was and continues to be the maintenance of an identity that feels satisfyingly authentic and secures for Navajo people an adequate degree of economic and political autonomy in the face of pervasive American domination. This dual task has required great determination along with subtlety and creativity. The difficulty is how to be enough like the dominant society to attract the profits and benefits of American identity while remaining different enough to secure a dissimilar set of profits and benefits from Navajo tribal status.

Navajos have addressed this challenge by using two contrasting approaches. On one hand, they have accepted elements from the dominant society and, indeed, have become functioning members of it to varying degrees. This assimilation or accommodation, to whatever extent it is achieved, has allowed many Navajos to take advantage of the resources and benefits that accrue to their identity as unmarked American citizens—persons who have conformed to American expectations of citizens.

On the other hand, most Navajos continue to exert some degree of resistance to "melting" into the dominant American way of being—which has many negative associations growing out of generations of exclusion, denigration, and pain. This resistance may be slight or quite resolute; in either case, it leads individuals and the Navajo people as a whole to create and frequently to live an identity that is powerfully different from, even oppositional to, that of mainstream American society. American colonization of North America has always been met with resistance from its indigenous inhabitants. Among Navajos, such resistance has taken many forms, ranging from remarkably effective military counteroffensives in the days before the Long Walk to the rejection of Collier's stock reduction plan in the 1930s. This resistance to American domination has also been expressed in the retention of pre-American Navajo cultural traits—language, "traditional" ceremonialism, the clan and kinship system, and material elements. In addition, resistance has been and continues to be expressed in the creation of new and innovative constructions and institutions for Navajos—a sense of pan-Indianism and, more recently, a sense of identification with other indigenous groups, the wide-ranging Native American Church, and Navajo nationalism.

HEGEMONY AND COUNTERHEGEMONY

The inequality of power between the United States and the Navajos can be better understood using the political theory of Antonio Gramsci (1971), with elaborations and modifications by the literary theorist Raymond Williams (1977). Whereas traditional definitions of hegemony emphasize direct political or military coercion working upon a subordinated group through state and civil institutions, Williams (1977:108) underscored the distinction between "rule," as direct or effective coercion, and "hegemony." As Susan Philips (1998:8) has noted, hegemony is "the consent of the governed through ideological persuasion." She continues: "For Gramsci, hegemony was never complete; the struggle of the state to maintain the consent of the governed is constant" (Philips 1998:11). The citizenry's consent may be gained and maintained in a variety of ways. Williams (1977:112, 115–116) described the workings of hegemony through "selective tradition," the contemporary construction of a version of the past in which certain meanings and practices are selected for emphasis at the expense of others. This is a means of fashioning a "traditional" past, and therefore a future, that furthers the interests of the dominant class. Simultaneously, other factions within the state exert unceasing resistance and pressure for change motivated by their own self-interest.

In the United States Southwest, this selective reshaping was originally formulated by American government policymakers, business entrepreneurs, and religious leaders as an epic battle between good and evil, between desirable progress and civilization brought by brave and adventurous pioneers and the obsolete and objectionable savagery of the region's indigenous inhabitants, including the Navajos. This radically selective historicization of early contact between Navajos and Westerners and of the period that followed it was and continues to be used to justify and organize the conquest and subsequent oppression of native North Americans.

The United States' version of its acquisition of the western portion of North America, as represented by its own selective tradition, is vulnerable to challenge. It is, as Williams (1977:116) pointed out, "vulnerable because the real record is effectively recoverable, and many of the alternative or opposing practical continuities are still available." In the U.S. Southwest, the indigenous tribal groups who were displaced or contained by American military and political actions are still around, and they provide a different and challenging account of their encounter with the West. They have demonstrated their determination to "resist, limit, alter, and challenge" the state's hegemony. The forces that express this resistance represented for Williams (1977:112–113) concepts of counterhegemony and alternative hegemony. These two resistant ideological hegemonies are distinguished by the fact that counterhegemony assumes its shape in opposition to the dominant hegemony it is resisting, whereas alternative hegemony does not.

Therefore, we can see that within any culture or ethnic or national group, the dynamic cultural process that is hegemonic includes ideological subsections that can and do struggle and resist incorporation through a mixture of counterhegemonic and alternative strategies (Williams 1977:113). The result is a society that (like all societies) exhibits a range of hegemonic, counterhegemonic, alternative hegemonic, and mixed ideological positions at any given time.

For the Navajo Nation, there is no question that the United States' military conquest, continued domination, and supposed incorporation of the Navajo people into the country's citizenry is the hegemony of a state over a subject people. It is equally clear that Navajos exert a strong counterhegemonic force—often rejecting a singular "American" identity and disparaging "mainstream" values and ideals. Their continued practice and assertion of their distinctive traditional character may take counterhegemonic or alternative forms or both, depending on the context and on whether practices and representations are being held up as oppositional to a loathed and disvalued hegemony.

For many generations, Navajos have retained an unusually large measure of their indigenous language, culture, and beliefs in comparison with other Native American groups. A great majority of the Navajo population remained concentrated in relative isolation in their own homeland and legal reservation between their own sacred mountains. However, with the advent of military service and jobs associated with World War II, the funding of government education and health programs, the expansion of paved roads and media, continued Christian proselytizing, and so on, the Navajos were drawn ever farther into the mainstream of American practices. This process can be recognized as the gradual hegemonic incorporation of the Navajo people through American state and civil institutions: the military, schools, state and federal public services, and religious entities. Predictably, the incorporation has been only partial. Some Navajos, especially elders who continue to live in isolated rural settings, who often remain monolingual speakers of Navajo, and who continue to practice the traditional culture they grew up with, can be characterized as relatively unincorporated due to their allegiance to an alternative hegemony.

Other Navajos have adopted a variety of counterhegemonic resistance strategies. The means by which some of these have been formulated and put into practice reflect the same sort of selective references to tradition that went into the formulation of the hegemonic strategies. Again, specific meanings and practices are selected for emphasis or exclusion; they provide a useful vision of a glorious and honorable past, and they provide a "historical" model or a set of tools for constructing a similarly proud and satisfying present and future. This counterhegemonic selective tradition indexes the same dichotomy that served the hegemonic state, but it reverses the values of the poles. In this figuration, the dominant group is bad, their victims good (Clifton 1989; Krupat 1992).

Many of these counterhegemonic assertions and projections have met with a great deal of approbation and validation, not only in Navajo settings but elsewhere in the United States and in other Western countries. For instance, the belief in a long-standing sacred and spiritual connection between Navajos and their land (known as Diné Bikéyah and sometimes Dinétah—the land between the sacred mountains) is a key element in Navajo self-identification. The assertion of many generations of intact cultural tradition challenges anthropological claims of the Navajos' relatively recent arrival in the Southwest. It bolsters the Navajos' position in their legal conflict with the Hopis, who want to reclaim portions of this territory where they, too, have lived for centuries. Furthermore, the divine origin of the clan system, the Navajo language, and Navajo cultural teachings and lifestyle, granted as gifts to the Diné by the Holy People, are continually underlined as essential to the Navajos' persistence as a people.

Certain prophesies connect these traditional beliefs with the future of the Navajos as Navajos and with the well-being of the universe. As Della Toadlena, an instructor at Diné College, said, "a long time ago, a prophesy was made that if we ever stopped talking Navajo, if we stopped, you know, if we forgot our language, then that would be the end of the Navajo Nation, of the Navajo culture" (September 27, 1994). Johnson Dennison, a well-known medicine man from the Round Rock community and dean of the West Campuses of Diné College when this research was conducted, explained the importance of the Navajo language in a larger context. He said that Navajos and their language are important parts of the universe; if the Navajos ever ceased to speak their language, a part would be missing and the universe would be thrown off balance, perhaps with unfortunate consequences (June 1, 1994).

When these beliefs and teachings are recruited from Navajo tradition to bolster and justify resistance or opposition to hegemonic incorporation—for example, to justify the development of educational programs to teach Navajo language and culture in an increasingly English-speaking and Western-dominated Navajo world—they are clearly counterhegemonic.

Interestingly, many of the aspects of Navajo culture that remain have been permitted, and in recent years even encouraged, by the United States government. They have served to give the Navajos the sense that their distinct cultural identity is intact. Donna Deyhle (1995:424) concurs with this assessment, writing: "Traditional Navajo cultural values still frame, shape, and guide appropriate behavior in the Navajo community." Her description of features of Navajo governmental structure are intended to support that contention:

> Unique to this governmental structure is the infusion of Navajo culture. Traditional home sites that are determined by sheep and cattle grazing rights are maintained by a Land Permit Office; a tribal court system relies on a Navajo legal code, as well as a federal legal code; the Navajo Medicine Men's Association is housed in the complex of the tribal headquarters, with an office at the local hospital; all significant tribal meetings are prefaced with a traditional prayer from a Medicine Man; and [the] Navajo Nation publishes its own newspaper to provide a Navajo perspective on local and national matters. In 1986, 286 retail businesses, 94 of them Navajo owned, operated on the reservation. The Navajo Communication Company provides cable television and telephones to homes with electricity, and the Native American Public Broadcasting Consortium provides local news to radio listeners. (Deyhle 1995:424)

To Deyhle, the foregoing is evidence of Navajo resistance to assimilation and their survival with "a culture that, although changed, has remained distinct in its values, beliefs, and practices" (1995:424). My interpretation is different. I am happy to concede that distinctive Navajo values, beliefs, and practices still exist among the Navajo Nation. I concur that there are individuals who still live by these elements. Where Deyhle and I part company is in our representations of the extent to which this ancestral cultural complex still characterizes the Navajo people as a whole. While acknowledging that "there are hundreds of different ways of 'being' Navajo," Deyhle (1995:425) also writes, "However, within this cultural constellation, specific values are maintained." My research has given me the impression that a significant segment of the Navajo population—certainly more than a few individuals, families, or other groupings—is unfamiliar with and does not adhere to even the most basic traditional values, beliefs, and traditions. I believe this painful realization lies at the heart of the outpouring of impassioned discourses concerning the importance and necessity of Navajo language and culture. I believe it stands behind the creation of myriad Navajo language and culture programs and celebrations.

Rather than interpreting the many Navajo civil and state institutions operating on the reservation—including those representing government, schooling, health care, media, and business—as evidence of clear Navajo control, I interpret them as reflecting the relatively superficial Navajo-ization of what are essentially Western institutions.

Manifestations of the Navajo-ization of tribal institutions include, among other things, the development of the bilingual school programs, assertions of political sovereignty, and the eventual establishment (despite initial rejection during the era of the Indian Reorganization Act of 1934) of "Navajo" executive, legislative, and judicial branches of government. However Navajo these institutions may appear, it must be recognized that these forms of self-assertion have posed no significant threat to United States domination and control; they have been subject to a sort of hegemonic containment. For instance, most of these institutions are transparently modeled on Western originals, and their power and influence are limited and defined for them by the federal government and the Department of the Interior. This is not to deny that Navajos have made a considerable effort to mask this element of the United States' indulgence.

This description of the pervasive power of the hegemonic state over the Navajos is not meant to belittle the Navajo Nation and its accomplishments. Rather, my intention is to show that the state asserts itself in insidious and hidden ways—as in the structure of institutions that appear and are identified as Navajo yet are, at their core, almost wholly Western. Additionally, negotiation and struggle over political, social, and economic control of the Navajos and their resources are ongoing.

One of the sites where the interaction between hegemonic and counterhegemonic forces can be clearly seen is Navajo schools. Although some of the mechanisms are more easily recognized in the past, most of the same forces are in play today.

Language, often in the context of schooling, is another major site where hege-

mony acts. It exerts a powerful force on decisions about which language (or variety of language) is valued, which one is merely tolerated, and which is expected
or required for what purpose. The hegemonic power controls certain domains and
specifies what will be accepted and what will be judged appropriate. For example,
in the United States, some form of "standard" English is required for most formal
speaking and writing tasks, for schooling, and for many jobs. That some Navajos
have internalized judgments about its social value and functionality has been made
clear to me in conversations and class discussions with a number of Navajos. Firsthand I have heard Navajos describe this "standard" variety as more "professional,"
"courteous," "effective," and "logical" than Navajo for the institutional settings
and purposes mentioned above. I have also heard Navajo educators enrolled in
teacher education programs at Northern Arizona University and Arizona State University label their own and their students' varieties of English as "slang," "bad English," "substandard," "confusing," and "not really a language."

The state's hegemony acted on language among the Navajos in similar ways in
the past. It was only in trading contexts—where the ultimate goal was the trader's
economic profit—and in some churches that Anglos were at all likely to learn, use,
and value the Navajo language as a medium of routine communication.

Early boarding schools were particularly notorious for forbidding the use of the
Navajo language. Students who violated this policy were often subjected to ugly
and degrading punishments, such as having their mouths "washed out" with harsh
lye soap or being made to stand with heavy dictionaries balanced at the end of
their outstretched arms. The overtly assimilationist agenda of such schools was
to remake the identity of Navajo children—to destroy and replace the Navajo identity they brought to school with them. Furthermore, as many as possible of the outward signs of students' Navajo identities were erased and replaced with Western
elements. Garments worn from home were removed and destroyed, to be replaced
by military-like "uniforms." Long hair in the *tsiiyééł,* the traditional hair bun, was
chopped into a short bob for girls and a military cut for boys; turquoise earrings
were removed and the pierced holes allowed to grow shut. Students were forbidden to speak Navajo in public and in the dormitories. Yet even when this transformation appeared to be complete, Navajo (and other Native American) students
were still judged to be lacking. If they spoke only English, it was often characterized
as "bad" English. If they pursued employment in Anglo homes or other work sites,
they were placed primarily in domestic positions or hired for manual labor requiring physical strength and endurance and for tasks that were tedious and repetitive
(Trennert 1988).

The grip of the hegemonic state over these schools, however, was only partial;
there was also an active counterhegemony that resisted the schools' assimilation-

ist practices. Somehow, the Navajo language continued to be used. Frank Morgan, a former cultural specialist in the Diné Educational Philosophy Office at Diné College, described his own experiences at the BIA Boarding School in Farmington, New Mexico: "If you were caught speaking Navajo [in the dorm], you were put on what they called a black list, and all your privileges, movies, whatever, that was taken away for at least a week. So you were grounded for speaking any Navajo. So you had to sneak around to talk Navajo. But most of us, every time we communicated, it was all in Navajo" (August 29, 1994).

Alternatively, some students boldly spoke their language in the face of strong disapproval and accepted their punishment. The insistence of Navajo and other Native American students that their language had to remain an important element in their identity can be seen as part of a larger resistance by such students. In addition to continuing to speak their language either publicly or in secret, students resisted assimilation and subjugation in a variety of ways. Several books focusing on Indian children's experiences at Indian boarding schools (Adams 1995; Lomawaima 1994; McBeth 1983; Trennert 1988), as well as autobiographies of Indians who attended boarding schools (Qoyawayma 1964; Sekaquaptewa 1969; Shaw 1974; Stewart 1980; Yava 1978), provide us with much information regarding this sort of resistance.

IDEOLOGIES ASSOCIATED WITH HEGEMONIC POSITIONS

To better underscore the multiple ideological connections between the exercise of hegemony and the acceptance or rejection of that hegemony, I turn to the work of Lila Abu-Lughod (1991), who explains that we can no longer productively conceive of groups (her example is the Bedouins) as "cultures" in the time-honored sense of this word. Instead, she suggests that we speak of ideological positions found within ethnic groups, a usage that recognizes the diversity within these groups. Abu-Lughod's rejection of the term "culture" (1991:144) is also based on the fact that "the anthropological distinction between self and other rests on it. Culture is the essential tool for making other. As a professional discourse that elaborates on the meaning of culture in order to account for, explain, and understand cultural difference, anthropology also helps construct, produce, and maintain it. Anthropological discourse gives cultural difference (and the separation between groups of people it implies) the air of the self-evident."

I would claim that among the Navajos (and other Native American groups), the present-day sense of a distinct Navajo identity (that is, a sharp distinction between Navajo selves and others) is in great part predicated on the use—with minimal adaptations—of the very criteria that have traditionally been cited by anthropologists to "account for, explain, and understand cultural difference." Whereas these distinguishing features were, of course, initially observed among and learned from Navajos themselves, they are not always visible in the lives of contemporary Navajos. For instance, in Navajo culture classes at Diné College and Northern Arizona University, which serve Navajo as well as non-Navajo students, Navajo instructors routinely use standard anthropological texts and disciplinary jargon to describe and name traditional Navajo practices and characteristics. This self-representation is another site where contemporary Navajo identity is defined according to categories and features foregrounded by hegemonic institutions. It is ironic that as Western anthropology rejects such essentializing (that is, Orientalizing) as inaccurate and damaging, Navajos, among others, have embraced what Abu-Lughod (1991:144) terms "reverse Orientalism." This occurs "when attempts to reverse the power relationship proceed by seeking to valorize for the self what in the former system had been devalued as other." She continues: "While turning [these stereotypes] on their heads, they preserve the rigid sense of difference based on culture."

Regardless of who practices such essentializing, it is "a reduction of someone from a particular group to the stereotypes, negative or positive, [that] we have of that group" (Chow 1994:125). What is at issue here is the notion that members, as well as observers, of a particular group have become invested in a "politics of identifying 'authentic' natives" and have asked questions such as "How do we identify the native? How do we identify with her? How do we construct the native's 'identity'? What processes of identification are involved?" (Chow 1994:126). Ultimately, when these difficult questions receive short, facile answers, the result of scrutiny of the "natives" and their perceived predicament is less, rather than greater, understanding.

Such essentialisms may come into existence, however, for a very serious reason, one that must not be trivialized or silenced because the people who are confronted with an ugly picture of themselves are uncomfortable or resentful. As bell hooks (1995:37–38) put it, "I want to focus on the representation of whiteness that is not formed in reaction to stereotypes but emerges as a response to the traumatic pain and anguish that remain a consequence of white racist domination, a psychic state that informs and shapes the way black folks 'see' whiteness." She went on to say, "African Americans have learned oppositional ways of thinking that enhance our capacity to survive and flourish" (hooks 1995:57). And finally: "That was a formulation that was necessary at a particular point in time, when we were still within the whole identity crisis, when we were trying to evolve a peoplehood" (hooks 1995:249). These points certainly apply to Navajo experience as well.

But although these essentializations may be "provisionally useful in forging a sense of unity and in waging struggles of empowerment," as Abu-Lughod (1991: 145) claimed, there comes a time when effective social action and individual agency require that intragroup diversity be recognized. As hooks (1995:247) explained it: "The contemporary crisis of identity is best resolved by our collective willingness as African Americans to acknowledge that there is no monolithic black community, no normative black identity. There is a shared history that frames the construction of our diverse black experiences. Knowledge of that history is needed by everyone as we seek to construct self and identity."

We know that the essentialized images of "natives" (as well as their others) that are constructed through oppositions are tidier, easier to manipulate for strategic ends, and easier to characterize in simplistic (and therefore at least partially false) ways. Ideologies associated with these polarized stances and essentialized identities in competitions for power, status, and resources may also be naively represented; they are attached to either the dominant group or the subordinated, even victimized, group. However, the very naturalness and obviousness with which these "sides" are characterized as oppositional obscures the complex identities, diverse personal and group goals, and varied lifestyle choices and ambitions held by individuals and subgroups. And until this diversity, as well as the ideological contestation and conflict that it implies, is unflinchingly recognized, complex issues and critical problems—such as the swift decline of the Navajo language—will be underestimated, inadequately explained, and insufficiently addressed.

THE BENEFITS
OF BEING AMERICAN

The political relationship between the contemporary United States and the Navajos is more complex and dynamic than one might think. Navajos do not act as a uniform group; neither do they all hold the same attitudes and beliefs about the dominant society. Rather than uniformly accepting *or* rejecting this source of power and control, Navajo society exhibits a simultaneous attraction to and repulsion by elements of the dominant culture. The result is a confusing and contradictory individual and group sense of what it is to be Navajo at the beginning of the twenty-first century. Navajos, individually and as a people, are therefore engaged in a sort of ideological engineering. They are working to be recognized as a sovereign and autonomous political nation and, at the same time, to craft a Navajo identity as a complex, dignified, and culturally and spiritually rich people.

In order to deconstruct the complex ideological circumstances that I have observed in contemporary Navajo ways of life, I have taken up the concepts of "mimesis" and "alterity" as they are discussed by Michael Taussig (1993). His work, though not specifically about Navajos, provides a valuable theoretical perspective for recognizing that contemporary Navajos are attempting, in many ways, to be mainstream Americans while concurrently maintaining their distinctive Navajo identity. In other words, they are attempting simultaneous mimesis (sameness) and alterity (differentness)—a difficult challenge that results in considerable individual and tribal ideological diversity, contradiction, and conflict. It is a demanding undertaking; its conflicting claims lie, I believe, at the root of the Navajos' present-day struggle over their aboriginal language, culture, and identity.

The assertion that Navajos want—sometimes and in some ways—to be the same as mainstream Americans is a controversial claim. After all, Navajos have so many reasons for wanting to be anything *but* like their conquerors and oppressors. Yet there is ample evidence in the practices of Navajo people to support the claim that Navajos and their Navajo culture are becoming increasingly "the same" as mainstream Americans and their "culture." How and why is this happening?

When so much of contemporary Navajo practice appears to be voluntarily Western in unrecognized and unacknowledged ways, it is clear that long-term and persistent hegemonic incorporation has taken place. Through this process, Navajo-ness has been influenced, shaped, and—it would be no exaggeration to say—reinvented. To underscore the fact that truly successful incorporation results in the apparent naturalness and inevitabilty of elements and institutions of the hege-mony, we have only to look at aspects of contemporary Navajo "traditional" identity that have Western (that is, Spanish and American) origins. These include the im-portance of livestock (sheep, goats, and cattle) and the pastoral lifestyle. That Navajo oral history now explains the origin and care of livestock as part of an authentic, precontact Navajo-ness provides incontrovertible evidence of the whole-hearted acceptance of livestock into the Navajo way of life.

One version of this origin story says that when the first Navajo people created by Changing Woman accompanied her back from the home that the Sun had made for her in the west, they were formed into clans. Males and females from different clans were paired by Changing Woman so that they could marry. She instructed them in how to behave. At the same time, she provided for these couples by making horses, sheep, cattle, and donkeys from fetishes. She placed the fetishes in four directions in a basket and covered it with an unwounded buckskin. Each time she lifted the buckskin, one of the fetishes came to life. The resulting four animals were then given to humans. Changing Woman also gave each of these animals a song, and the songs are now part of the Blessing Way ceremony (Harry Walters, December 14, 1995).

Other such Western items and practices that have become core elements in traditional Navajo life are dietary staples such as mutton and fry bread made of wheat flour (both introduced by the Spaniards). Additionally, weaving in wool, sil-versmithing and other metal working, Western studio art of the sort practiced by Harrison Begay, Clifford Beck, and R. C. Gorman, flounced skirts and velveteen blouses for women, the manufacture of sand paintings on masonite boards, and pickup trucks are rarely thought or spoken of as Western. Though all these ele-ments have mimetic origins, they are now different enough to feel alteric, and therefore they are appropriate items or practices to carry counterhegemonic ideo-logical weight.

Certain other typical "Navajo" events now common to the Navajo Nation are also Western in origin but have been given a distinctly Navajo cast. Rarely is the Western origin mentioned. Such events include the public teaching of traditional knowledge in Western-style workshops, seminars, in-service training sessions, and

college classes. In addition to disseminating traditional knowledge, these activities are also sources of cash income for the sponsoring institutions and the presenters.

Further activities that openly use "traditional" productions as commodities
are fund-raisers of various kinds staged in support of Diné College student clubs
(the Red Dawn Indian Club, the Native American Church of Diné College), families
with medical emergencies or pressing financial needs, public-school field trips and
graduations, and Nationwide organizations such as the Navajo Arts and Humani-
ties Council. Fund-raisers include raffles with Navajo-made or Navajo-associated
crafts and objects (silver and turquoise jewelry, Pendleton blankets, pottery, sheep,
weavings) as prizes; Native American Church raffles with NAC paraphernalia going
to the winners; "traditional song-and-dances" and powwows with cash prizes;
food sales featuring Navajo tacos, mutton stew or sandwiches, and fry bread; and
concerts and other performing arts (music, dance, storytelling, comedy, poetry
reading). Additional fund-raisers are sports events including rodeos and related
livestock events such as bull-dogging contests and woolly riding competitions (in
which Navajo youngsters attempt to ride long-haired sheep and goats). There are
also basketball games (the reservation has been described by Tsaile resident Nancy
Mike as "basketball heaven") that pit the Navajo Nation executive staff against
KTTN radio station employees, or Diné College faculty against students. A final and
unique type of fund-raiser is something called "squaw basketball," in which male
basketball players dress up in traditional-style Navajo women's clothing and play a
lively burlesque version of basketball.

Although the presence of such elements in Navajo life might at first glance
seem trivial, upon closer examination and deeper thought it can be seen clearly
as part of a metamorphosis in the Navajo economy. The Navajos were transformed
from a scattering of mobile hunting and gathering bands into more sedentary pas-
toralists who were drawn into a capitalist economy through trade in sheep and
related products (mutton, wool, and weaving), silversmithing, and art. Furthermore, although the period before and after the American conquest saw Navajo men
and women captured and forced to work as slaves in Mexican, New Mexican, and
American homes, Navajos eventually began to work away from their homes and
families for cash wages. All of the productions and activities just described are evidence of Navajo economic incorporation.

These practices have also required that Navajos become consumers in this
economy—buying cowboy boots, jeans, and saddles, Blue Bird flour and Hormel
lard for fry bread, raw materials for silversmithing, and fabric and sewing machines
to produce "traditional" clothing. The list could go on and on.

Another quite overt level of hegemonic incorporation is the Navajos' controversial adoption of Western bureaucratic institutions and structures (mostly schools and governmental offices) and social patterns such as male dominance and top-down leadership. These are much more likely to be consciously recognized as Western and, therefore, to be openly suspect. As Benjamin Barney, then director of the Diné Teacher Education Program, said, "I think today they use school board members and Navajo administrators kind of as a front, but I have a feeling some of their policies are still the same way" (September 1, 1994). Ferlin Clark also touched on this issue, saying, "And you have to look at how these schools are structured, and how they came about. It's not by Navajos, you know. The whole thing was assimilation" (February 6, 1995).

On one hand, Navajos are certainly conscious of their history of domination and of the many overt ways in which power has been exerted over their social lives, political structures, language, religion, public education, and so on. These are the areas in which Navajos have consciously resisted via counterhegemonic strategies, and these are the areas that are well covered in discourse.

Yet despite (or in addition to) the elements of resistance to and rejection of incorporation, there is also evidence of deliberate, cautious, and strategic acceptance of elements of hegemonic incorporation. Underlying the adoption of Western social and political institutions and practices, therefore, are very Western social values—progress, success, individualism, materialism, comfort, and convenience—that are appealing to many Navajos.

The adoption of these values has repercussions and consequences for many traditional aspects of Navajo life. Certain Western practices follow from the adoption of these values and must be consciously undertaken in order to secure Western-style benefits. These practices include pursuit of comparatively well-paying and stable jobs and careers; competition in place of routine cooperation and sharing; adoption of Western-style clothing, hairdressing, and cosmetics; use of the English language and associated verbal routines; emphasis on the nuclear family rather than the extended, or clan, family; and pursuit of formal education and degrees. Such strategies, when "successful," result in material and monetary surpluses as a mark of success; multiroom houses with plumbing and electricity, furniture, appliances, and electronic entertainment equipment; physical mobility via vehicles and paved roads; improved communication—by telephone and e-mail; information access by means of radio, television, and the Internet, and so on. This is the area in which deliberate Western "mimesis" is taking place in the present-day lives of Navajos. And this is the area in which we must return to the question implied earlier: Why "choose" to be like one's oppressors and conquerors?

A clue is found in Taussig's (1993:xiii–xiv) description of the "mimetic faculty" that is available to members of a culture. This faculty includes the ability of an individual or an institution to copy or imitate an original and thus to draw on and even assume the character and power of the original. When we ask, "Why mimic?" a possible answer is that by being a copy of an other, by yielding into and becoming an other who has a desirable character and power, one assumes that very character and power oneself. Therefore, we might say that Navajos mimic Anglos (the dominant figures in the ongoing political struggle) in specific areas and strategic ways in order to gain greater access to the attractive features of Anglo lives—material wealth, power, and independence.

The existence of mimicry as a strategy to exert agency in Navajo lives is not difficult to demonstrate. Following their agonizing military defeat and subsequent political and cultural domination by Americans, the Navajos entered a new era in their history. Many aspects of their lives that they had taken for granted—the freedom to come and go as they wished, the lack of centralized authority and control over their autonomous bands, the exclusive right of family and clan elders to make decisions about socialization and education—had now come under the control of the United States government. To be subordinate is, by definition, to have lost control and authority over one's life. Navajos were faced with the challenge of building on their traditional practices in order to attain once again a degree of control over their lives.

Traditionally, Navajos already had sacred beliefs and rituals that provided not only comfort and psychological security but also a sense of control over an unpredictable and ungovernable world. Indeed, the whole point of most Navajo ceremonies is to re-create the world as it was meant to be—that is, characterized by harmony, balance, and health. These ceremonies not only heal the physical bodies of people but also work as a sort of traditional "imitative magic" to restore individuals, groups, and the world in general to an ideal state. This is done through the retelling of the Emergence story—a whole sequence of events and teachings that gradually brought the Navajo world into being and into harmony in the first place. Recounting this sequence of events (or portions of the sequence) calls on imitative magic to produce in people and other aspects of nature the same order as that evoked in the narrative.

This brief view of how Navajos utilize mimicry in traditional ways to influence outcomes in their lives leads to an examination of how contemporary Navajos use another form of mimicry or mimesis to understand and deal with the complex relations of domination and subordination between them and Anglo society, particularly in the area of language. In that regard, Navajos' coping behaviors are shaped by the specific linguistic ideologies they hold about relations between the Navajo language and English. Evidence of the hegemonic and associated ideology or ideologies held by Navajos can be heard in their discourse and seen in their actions.

In their relations with the United States (past and present), in which the dominant society clearly has the upper hand, Navajos have come to appropriate a degree of power and control over their own lives via mimesis. Their use of mimetic "rituals"—the copying of targeted Western behaviors and appearances—may attract, secure, and maintain a greater degree of practical control over their own lives.

Most Navajos appear to be critical of the consequences of being "like the white man." One hears few positive statements about being this way, and those few are likely to be made in private, protected settings. For instance, in discussing the fact that few Navajos, if any, live exclusively "traditional" lifestyles today, Frank Morgan told a class I was enrolled in that even "a medicine man likes electricity in his house. He gets the blessing from it" (March 7, 1995). This was part of a discussion about the fact that there are Navajo teachings about recognizing positive things from the outside and attracting them to you, but needing to be careful so that they are not used in an excessive or bad way.

In addition, Della Toadlena said that "based on the Sa'ąh Naagháí Bik'eh Hózhóón concept, one common goal that we all cater to is to one day live a good, successful life and to Navajos, to many Navajos, that means having a job, having a good-paying job, having a nice vehicle, having a nice home. So everybody aspires to stuff like that or they want to have stuff like that" (September 27, 1994).

One such characteristic behavior of a dominant group that may be thought to offer practical value and advantage to members of a subordinate group is the learning and appropriate use of its language. My speech data show that many Navajos hold clear-cut language ideologies that assign English a tremendous weight in securing them "success" in professional, educational, and other Western settings. That Navajos mark English as a language associated with access to power, status, respect, prestige, and economic benefits in both professional and private life is clear in the discourse of Navajos. They often speak of decisions made by parents as they raise their children: "When you're growing up, I was always told, by my parents, too, 'Learn English, learning English, learn everything you can about it, and that's the only way you can become successful'" (Ferlin Clark, February 6, 1995). "Most Navajo families are thinking English is a dominant language, the work the kids will encounter will be in English; therefore, they think by giving them an early start, whether it's correct English or what, nevertheless, they're on their way, you know, to that. So I think that people are thinking in those terms, you know, economics and so, they in their mind, some sort of stability for their kids. So, you know, I think that's why they're doing it" (Paul Willeto, May 22, 1994). "There must have been a time, and I know it was there because I've heard it before, where parents they decided not to teach their kids Navajo because they didn't want them to be unsuccessful or they wanted them to be more successful or more fluent in English and that same idea I guess from early age probably has been forced on them that, 'You got to learn it this way and this is the only way and you can't be thinking about your other way, otherwise it's going to hold you back,' kind of idea" (Celeste Charley [pseudonym], June 1, 1994).

They speak of the importance of English in professional settings: "I use English in almost every corner of my career at work, and [even] if I'm not at work, I communicate in English" (Johnson Dennison, June 1, 1994). "One of the things is that there's a sense of personal self and also a real sense of power and control that goes with language. Any language. And I think today in the Navajo world, in this society, you have to be pretty fluent in English. So the better you are at handling English, the opportunities of having to do many things are there. . . . If you don't articulate really well in English, I think you tend to be ignored in the meetings and many many events, not only in the school, but also outside. I think you limit yourself also in talking and sharing ideas with people that are not Navajo speaking. And so it's very important, I think" (Benjamin Barney, September 1, 1995). "[It is important to speak good English] because all business, transactions, education, all fields, you know, demands it, and to be able to read, understand English is very important" (Harry Walters, October 7, 1994). "There's a certain job that has to be done, I feel, and I speak mostly to them [co-workers and subordinates] in English so that it's clear. I think one reason why I do that is because of how I have to be clear about certain things, about asking them to do certain things specifically, and the Navajo language has limitations. That's why I don't use it a lot. You know, the Navajo language has a lot of limitation in terms of business, in the business environment" (Paul Willeto, May 22, 1994).

Humiliating and damaging social judgments are made when a Navajo speaks something other than standard English, as illustrated by Della Toadlena's account (September 27, 1994):

I think it's very important for Navajos to speak good English. . . . Some people will say, "I know enough to get by. That's all I need; it's not my first language anyway." And my husband will tend to say that, but I think that for the kids going to school, it's important. Well, one thing, one reason is that to avoid any embarrassment. Like, even now in class, when someone says something or something wrong or differently, everybody laughs, you know. To avoid something like that, you know, they should learn to speak it, I don't know, properly. I mean they can never be white people, but I think we should at least learn to speak it adequately at least so that it comes across, not as something that will be labeled later as, I don't know, Indian language, red language, or something like that.

Clothing and other elements of personal appearance, too, communicate hegemonic identification. One of the first changes made in the lives of new students in early federal boarding schools was to cut their hair and replace their own clothing with uniform Western clothing. Whether adopted voluntarily or not, the new clothing and hairstyle were perceived as outward signs of the wished-for transformation of Navajos (as well as other Indians at such boarding schools) into ordinary American citizens, ostensibly with the same rights and responsibilities as any others. Clothing and hairstyle, therefore, may often have ideological meanings or functions. When traditional clothing and *tsiiyééł* are worn by Navajos (with the possible exception of elders going about their everyday lives), they should be recognized as alteric and, in contemporary times, worn consciously to emphasize Navajo distinctiveness from Anglo society. In contrast, Western clothing and hairstyles—especially business suits and other "dress for success" garb—conform to Western values in order to attract positive public opinion, respect, and serious regard. For example, a past president of Diné College, Tommy Lewis, was well known within the college community for his insistence, documented in several "dress code" memos, on "professional" dress. The following memo illustrates his response to the wearing of denim jeans, blue chambray work shirts, and T-shirts by faculty and staff members:

> Last year on August 26, 1993, I wrote a memorandum to all employees of the college to pay utmost attention to proper attire as educators and professionals representing Navajo Community College, I would like to reiterate once more the following. . . . "As College President I want to stress very strongly my belief that dress and appearance in a work environment is very important. We work at an educational institution where academic standards and professionalism must be maintained at the highest level. We must show our professionalism at all times as we have students and the general public on our campuses every day. As educators, administrators and employees of the College, we are the role models for students. One way to show our professionalism is through our own character—with that comes good appearance and appropriate attires.
>
> "The flagrant and improper behavior of NCC employees will not be condoned or tolerated. Such misconduct is unacceptable and negatively reflects on the professionalism expected of Navajo Community College. Any employee who comes to work in unacceptable attire will be asked to comply with this directive. Your cooperation and compliance is requested. If you have a problem with this directive, please feel free to call me or come see me." (Memorandum to: All Faculty & Staff, Navajo Community College. Subject: Policies and Procedures: Dress Code. August 25, 1994)

Lewis himself invariably appeared at work in stereotypical Western business wear: conservative suits, ties, polished black dress shoes, and a short haircut.

Of course, there is an alternative form of "professional dress" that is commonly worn by both Native Americans (including Navajos) and Anglos in the western part of the United States. Characterized by both Native American and Western (in the sense of the dominant society) elements, this style, worn by both men and women, features conspicuous Indian jewelry (bola ties, belt buckles, bracelets, rings, and— less commonly for men—earrings) and cowboy boots. Men dressed in this fashion also often wear denim jeans or western-cut slacks and cowboy hats. With the exception of Tommy Lewis, this is the style favored by most male employees at Diné College. There, too, as in most other work settings on the Navajo Reservation, Navajo and other Indian-style jewelry is almost universal on women; cowboy boots are optional.

For some Navajos, another source of desire to mimic Anglos may be an integrative motivation—a desire to participate in the life of the outside community, driven by a sincere and personal interest in the people and culture represented by the outside group. Because this motivation is so unpopular, most discourse representing Anglos and Anglo culture in a sincerely admiring or positive way is muted or silenced. Navajos who do say positive things about Anglo society (or any society other than their own) may be seen as odd and even suspect, not as "real Navajos." It is not surprising that discourse about the desirability of life off the reservation, of Western performance arts, of cappuccino and chocolate croissants at Starbucks is comparatively rare and takes place in private social settings.

THE REVITALIZATION
OF NAVAJO CULTURE
THREE

The alteric aspect of Navajo identity is much more visible and public than is the mimetic in contemporary times; it, too, has its roots in Navajo historical experience. Early in Navajo-American contact, Navajo differentness from Americans was automatic and took no thought or effort, bolstered as it was by population size, isolation, and in-group reinforcement. The end of physical and cultural isolation due to improved roads and the vast and pervasive influence of Western media put a period on that era. In addition, political domination, both past and present, aimed at incorporating Navajos into mainstream American society as an unmarked group with no special or unique status or identity—no Navajo culture, no Navajo language, no Navajo land—but simply as United States citizens like all others. This campaign of incorporation sparked Navajo ideological resistance—a conscious determination to remain different from the interlopers. It is this conscious resistance that is the root of counterhegemonic and alteric strategies. Awareness of the United States' program of domination, including the destruction of native language and culture, provided what the Acoma poet and activist Simon Ortiz (1993) has called the motive for a "fight-back."

This refusal to be swallowed up has led to a cultural revitalization effort that stresses alteric strategies. The goal of this movement is to recover and communicate a proud and positive image of Navajo-ness—to Navajos themselves and to others. Two such strategies, which are organized by a metaphor of opposition, are the use of alteric discourse and narratives to develop and champion the image of distinctive and authentic Navajo-ness, and the Navajo-ization of Navajo institutions so that they are sites for both the creation and practice of Navajo-ness (Navajo culture and Navajo language). This metaphor and these strategies have played important roles in maintaining and transmitting Navajo culture and language in the present and will no doubt do so into the future. They have had some unexpected and, for the most part, unrecognized negative aspects as well.

CULTURAL
REVITALIZATION

Obviously, the Navajo Nation's ongoing cultural revitalization efforts are a recognition of and a response to its military conquest and subsequent domination by the United States, which brought poverty and cultural dissolution. The situation also produced pervasive and trying emotions for Navajos: humiliation at their powerlessness to resist Western military and cultural pressures, shame at the widespread, degrading stereotypes of Navajos and of Indians in general, and, ultimately, rage at the interminable assimilatory and demeaning demands of the United States and its institutions.

As we know, Navajos had options to choose from in responding to these demands and pressures. They could accept what was asked of them and adapt as best as they could; certainly, some did this. They accepted the irreversibility of their domination and counseled adoption of the Anglos' way of doing things— speaking English, sending their children to boarding schools for the "white man's" education, taking wage-paying jobs, being baptized in the Christian religion. As bell hooks (1995:28) has observed, individuals who have achieved something like economic and social parity with the dominant society are often "most eager to silence discussions of militant rage because they are not interested in fundamentally challenging and changing [the] white supremacist capitalist patriarchy. They simply want equal access to privilege within the existing structure." They have acquiesced to the pressures and promises of the hegemonic power.

Other Navajos consciously tried to balance the demands of the United States system with their own ways. This perspective was expressed by John Dick (1977:189), one of the founders of the Rough Rock Demonstration School. "Education," he asserted, "both Anglo and traditional, must go side by side. Our children need to learn both. Their history and their culture cannot die out. Our children need to look back and see how our people lived. Then they can compare, to see how much we have progressed."

More recently, some Navajos are recognizing that their current lifestyle has resulted in the rapid attrition of their Navajo language and culture. Many are talking about the need for conscious efforts to reverse this process, to bring back many of the traditional ways of doing things before they are lost for good. Ferlin Clark told me that Navajos "have to assume that responsibility and willingness to learn the Navajo language. I think it is too important for us not to." He added: "Know who you are and where you come from and, you know, learn as much as you can about the language and culture" (February 6, 1995). This opinion was echoed by educators, students, and a number of other Navajos. Alvina Tsosie, a Diné College graduate, described the process she went through before she awakened to the importance of her Navajo traditions:

> *I believe that young people today are losing perspective of themselves as Navajos. I know this because I was one of them. I used to believe that trying to be more Anglo than Navajo would get me ahead. I know now that I need both the Anglo and the Navajo ways to get where I want to go. Although I grew up being taught my traditional ways, I think television had a bigger impact on my early life. I think that's still the problem today. . . . I think young people have a hard time in school because of not only the curriculum, but because they don't know who they are. . . . Without knowing their culture or language, children will never have a full understanding of themselves. Older people always say that your clan is your identity or who you are as an individual. Without an understanding of one's culture and language, how will one know who he/she is and therefore children will not realize the purpose they were put on this earth. They won't really care what they do with their lives because they don't have a full identity of themselves. (October 8, 1994)*

Awareness of this sort has led to a generalized Navajo revitalization movement. Though such movements often spring from specific messianic religious or spiritual sources, they may also be more amorphous efforts aimed literally at bringing a confused and disorderly culture or group back on track—at "revitalizing" the elements that gave the group strength, purpose, and a positive orientation. Such movements are one way a society balances mimetic and alteric drives. The resulting amalgam of old and new elements provides a basis from which to challenge the authority of the hegemony's ideological domination and to reassert positive aspects of a group's history, culture, and image. The revitalization of the Navajo image, culture, and language has publicly and passionately emphasized and valorized the alteric. Furthermore, the work on Navajo-ness sparked by this revitalization includes making the new and improved Navajo image—as well as Navajo language and selected aspects of Navajo culture—a marketable asset to the Navajo people, as a nation and as individuals.

ORGANIZING ALTERITY: AN OPPOSITIONAL DICHOTOMY

Edward Said (1993:100) wrote that "all cultures tend to make representations of foreign cultures the better to master or in some way control them." Historically, not only have representations of Navajos themselves been negative, but these judgments have been extended to their language as well. Henry Shonerd (1990:194–195) explained that "the Navajo language (along with the other indigenous languages of the region) not only presented great problems for the European learner but was considered unfit for transmitting, even via interpreters, the most important Christian concepts."

This sort of representation was the norm for much of the first hundred years of Navajo involvement with the United States. It was typical of mainstream attitudes and practices toward Native Americans in general. The United States followed its devastating conquest of the Navajo people with the imposition of governmental structures that supplanted or diminished many of the Navajos' traditional social institutions. Moreover, the United States has continued to exert its power to define and its authority to make such definitions a basis for Navajo policy into the present day. This is but another technique for completing the demoralization and pacification of an enemy.

Clearly, such an image of Navajos is damaging in many ways. Even today, Navajo youths and others are aware of the negative stereotypes that have come to be associated with their people. Ferlin Clark was confronted with these low expectations when he finished school: "So one day one of my uncles . . . challenged me, you know. He bet me two thousand that I wouldn't finish college. He bet me that I would come back, and return, become a drunk, and do construction work, you know, have kids, and just raise 'em in that fashion. I guess that's what's expected, you know; failure is expected, I guess, in that sense. And, um, success is really not, you know, something expected out of Navajos" (February 6, 1995).

Given such images and expectations, it is not surprising that a chief goal of a Navajo revitalization movement as a counterhegemonic project would be to reclaim a positive image of the Navajos, their culture, and their language. It is ironic, however, that the approach used for this adjustment retains the oppositional metaphor of the damaging American representations mentioned earlier. In the original "superior us" versus "inferior them" depictions, non-Indians saw Indians and Anglos as literally poles apart—as opposites—and values of good and bad were attached to each group, which supposedly was homogeneous ethnically, racially, and culturally. In other words, a diversity of features and characteristics was collapsed into narrow and rigid stereotypes. Of course, such essentializing and "good-bad" labeling is a common ethnocentric strategy for justifying political policies that privilege one group over another. Today, this ploy, as used in both the past and the present by American Anglos, is correctly recognized and labeled racist and unjust by a majority of Indians and non-Indians alike (Deyhle 1995).

In Navajo revitalization efforts of the last two decades of the twentieth century, as in most other contemporary Native American political endeavors, the opposition metaphor is intact, as is the notion of attaching "good-bad" labels to racial-ethnic-cultural stereotypes. The renovated dichotomous categories, however, reverse the values of the past in which whites were the "good guys"—cultured, civilized, honorable, religious, hardworking—and Navajos (like other Indians) were filthy, uncivilized, bloodthirsty savages lacking the Western work ethic. In this inverted dichotomizing, just as Indian and American people are good-bad opposites, so, too, are their cultures (including their values, beliefs, religious systems, institutions, and so on). Thus, Navajo (and Indian) cultures have come to be labeled by Navajos and some Anglos as infinitely superior to that of the greedy, materialistic, amoral Anglo society. Navajos are more spiritual, more in touch with the natural world, more humane, more balanced and harmonious. Della Toadlena expressed it this way: "What is white culture, other than what we see—computers, televisions, you know, skyscrapers, freeways? . . . [Without our language and culture], we would be like white people—bankruptcy, crime, violence, disease, rape, domestic violence, dysfunctional families" (September 27, 1994).

Turning the tables on the oppressor sounds very attractive as a resistance technique. In a discussion of displaced identities in the context of conquest and domination, Rey Chow (1994:136) reminds us of the anti-imperialist "desire for revenge—to do to the enemy *exactly* what the enemy did to him, so that colonizer and colonized would meet eye to eye." Adopting and reversing the values attached to the same cultural or racial categories used by whites in earlier times and turning them to Navajo purposes is a resistance strategy that has had the consequence, in many cases, of extending and validating the prevalent—in practice if not in theory— national policy of rejecting multiculturalism and human equality. This aspect of the reversed stereotypes is usually ignored. Navajos and non-Navajos alike appear rather comfortable with the massive effort that has been invested, in American society, in engineering a stereotypical appearance of value-laden homogeneity on either side of the oppositional pair. So pervasive and accepted are these stereotypes and valuations on the Navajo Reservation that it is not uncommon at public events for the opening "joke" in politicians' and orators' speeches to be a pointed comment about the moral, spiritual, physical, and other deficiencies of "the white man."

Describing the impetus behind such stereotyping, bell hooks (1995:38) wrote: "Stereotypes, however inaccurate, are one form of representation. Like fictions, they are created to serve as substitutions, standing in for what is real. They are there not to tell it like it is but to invite and encourage pretense. They are a fantasy, a projection onto the Other that makes them less threatening. Stereotypes abound where there is distance. They are an invention, a pretense when one knows that the steps that would make real knowing possible cannot be taken or are not allowed."

Similarly, teacher training materials for Navajo and other Indian schools characterize generic "Native Americans" in ways such as the following: "The group is all important"; "Respect for the wisdom of the elderly"; "Passive, modest. Let others dominate"; "Respect nature. Do not disturb balance." European Americans are their opposite: "The individual is all important"; "Promote your own welfare"; "Emphasis on youth"; "Assertive, confident, doer. Dominate"; "Acquire, save. Possessions bring status. Wealth and security sought after." In the book *Teaching the Native American,* in a chapter titled "Emphasizing the Positive Aspects of the Culture," Jon Reyhner (1992:38) provides 33 such oppositional pairs.

The abstract values expressed in such training materials are put into practice in Navajo classrooms. At Diné College, I frequently observed that non-Navajo students (Anglo, Hispanic, and others) were encouraged to disparage their own upbringing and cultural experiences. Furthermore, their language, literature, religion, family life, and ethnic identities are routinely, and at times painfully, denigrated and devalued by Navajo and non-Navajo instructors, administrators, and other students. This sort of extremism is not uncommon in such settings. Said (1993:xxvi) described this sort of practice: "Defensive, reactive, and even paranoid nationalism is, alas, frequently woven into the very fabric of education, where children as well as older students are taught to venerate and celebrate the uniqueness of *their* tradition (usually and invidiously at the expense of others)."

The function of the "us-them" dichotomy in Navajo cultural revitalization is to valorize alterity with a vengeance. Navajo differentness from the "dominant society" is rarely depicted neutrally; rather, it has become superior in every conceivable way. Differentness *is* identity. In my spring 1997 "Introduction to Sociology" class at what was then Navajo Community College, I gave my students a homework assignment that asked them to identify themselves by ethnicity, "race," culture, language, and nationality. The majority of the students answered the question in the same way: Navajo, Navajo, Navajo, Navajo, and Navajo. For them, these categories were isomorphic—whether they knew the Navajo language or not, whether they were familiar with traditional Navajo cultural teachings or not, whether they practiced the traditional belief system or not. Of course, they were aware that they were technically American citizens, and they were familiar with the rights and claims of this citizenship, but it was not a nationality that was at the forefront of most students' essentialized and self-evident identity. For them, as for many Navajos, Navajos and Anglos have become absolute others, on the surface at least.

NEW IMAGES
OF NAVAJO-NESS

Chow (1994:126) states that "for many, the image is also the site of possible change." What is changing in Navajo cultural revitalization is the "spoiled" image, to use Erving Goffman's (1963) term, of Navajo identity, culture, and language. Here is where the stereotypes are reversed, and here is where additional points about the worth and excellence of the Navajo people, culture, and language are made. One such claim for the Navajo language, for instance, is the oft-repeated assertion among Navajos that the Navajo language "won" World War II (Parsons-Yazzie 1995:31, 37). Because of this belief, there is bitter chagrin among Navajos that the contributions of the "code talkers," Navajo soldiers who used a code based on the Navajo language in the Pacific theater, are not given adequate credit and respect.

James Clifton (1989:2) has described how the effort to reengineer stereotypes on the Indian side of the oppositional pair was assisted by the shift in their representation in the media in the later part of the twentieth century. "Since the 1950s, for instance," he wrote, "movies and television productions have no longer portrayed Indians as vision-seeking, horse-riding Plains nomads menacing unwary settlers, substituting instead more sympathetic images that display Indians as innocents, as despoiled underdogs." Ferlin Clark discussed his own perception of the role of the media in this change, saying, "There's a pride in the culture. There's a pride in the language and I think, you know, from 1992 onwards . . . after the *Dances with Wolves* it kind of changed an attitude a little, you know. And I think that's where media, you know, movies, music, dance, culture, can change people's perception. And I think Native Americans finally felt, 'Wow!' you know, 'It's now cool to be Native American.' And so that brought on a lot of this, and I think it's kind of spread like wildfire on the Navajo [Reservation]" (February 6, 1995).

These quoted passages indicate the two different directions taken in the revision of Navajo stereotypes. Either of the two images fits comfortably in the Navajo slot of common Navajo-Anglo oppositional pairing. The first of these images is that of Navajos as victims—the "despoiled underdogs," to use Clifton's term. The other is an image of Navajo cultural and ethnic pride, making it finally "cool" to be Native American. Likewise, each of these essentialized Navajo identities entails a specific, opposite, essentialized Anglo-American identity.

A victim identity is certainly not inappropriate for the Navajos. Like other Native American groups, they have experienced considerable American military and political coercion and force. A focus on this aspect of their experience with their conquerors has, in some cases, resulted in what Donald Bahr (1989) has called "Victimist . . . history."

Arnold Krupat (1992:21) emphasized that Indians can and do foreground their oppression at the hands of Americans deliberately as a strategy to call attention to the need to reform and redress long-standing wrongs. The effectiveness of this practice as a political strategy, however, should not call into question the truth of the basic underlying claims. Krupat wrote: "One may grant that not all Euramericans were rapacious, genocidal monsters, and that not all Indians were, in the purest and most absolute sense, their hapless, innocent victims; nonetheless, it seems to me beyond question that—all things considered—the indigenous peoples of this continent, along with African Americans, women, and many other groups, have overwhelmingly been more sinned against than sinning. . . . Some people *have* been hurt by others, and if that is not the only and most interesting thing to say, it most certainly remains something that still, today, can probably not be said too often."

There is copious evidence that Navajos do see themselves as victims of American policies, practices, and values—not only in terms of lives lost during the military conquest and Long Walk into captivity of the 1860s, but also in ways that continue into the present. There are problems with this victimist identity, however. First, not all Navajos would characterize their experiences with government institutions such as boarding schools, a usual site for claims of victimization, negatively. Several people I interviewed spoke approvingly of the benefits of boarding school discipline, of the rigor of the academic program, of the fulfilling social activities, and of the useful skills they learned. In addition, a number of interviewees said that they themselves were never forbidden to speak their language and did not feel that their culture was threatened, although these are standard charges leveled at boarding schools as a group. Furthermore, later programs have attempted and continue to attempt to implement Navajo language, history, and cultural instruction into school curricula.

Another problem with a Navajo focus on a victim identity is that it places Navajos in a passive role, as individuals or as a group unable to take responsibility or to exercise agency to change their own direction and history. Addressing this issue, bell hooks (1995:51) wrote of the necessity for people to beware of too willingly allowing themselves to be characterized as victims in order to draw public attention to the need to put an end to exploitation and oppression. "My repudiation of the victim identity," she said, "emerged out of my awareness of the way in which thinking of oneself as a victim could be disempowering and disenabling." Furthermore, hooks (1995:58) cautioned that "to name oneself a victim is to deny agency."

In addition, when a racial, ethnic, or cultural group such as the Navajos embraces the identity of perpetual victimhood and denies itself the power to begin to correct its situation, it is also fixing the identity of the Anglo other as that of eternal oppressor—as the holder of all control and authority. Representing the other as uniformly and irredeemably bad is to reject the possibility of alliances with and support from individuals or subgroups within that group. Such essentialized stereotyping on the basis of skin color or other simple attributes, now as in the past, is dehumanizing and disabling for both members of the oppositional pair.

The other common stereotypical image that makes up the Native American pole in current Anglo-versus-Native-American (including Navajo) oppositional pairs is that of being "cool" or—to put it a bit less informally—heroic, romantic, noble. The possibility for Native Americans to easily and consistently see themselves in positive roles and situations is long overdue. In Navajo education literature and discourse, deficiencies in self-esteem and individual and tribal pride are cited over and over again as chief stumbling blocks to any sort of academic, personal, or job-related success. Renae Walters, a former Diné College student, explained the advice she would give to young Navajos about the importance of knowing and being proud of their Navajo identity: "I would tell them, 'Don't be ashamed of who you are. Look for yourselves; find yourselves; appreciate yourselves. Don't just walk around and not know who you are. Go to your grandparents; find out what clans you are. Find out how your clan originated. And you know, feel good about yourself. Tell yourself that you love yourself and just shape up. . . . To walk in beauty, you have to love yourself first" (April 4, 1995).

Indians might also emphasize other aspects of their past, other representations of themselves, as a prelude to more productive ways of ameliorating their oppressed condition. And indeed, Navajos' insistence, in their oral narratives (especially those centering on the Long Walk), on seeing themselves as strong and culturally blessed—something proved by their ability to withstand all that they have been subjected to—offers just such a positive and productive self-image.

Of course, there is an alternative to essentializing, and that is to see the interrelationships among peoples, the complex and confusing mixed natures of individuals and groups. Said (1993:61) put it well:

> If I have insisted on integration and connections between the past and the present, between imperializer and imperialized, between culture and imperialism, I have done so not to level or reduce differences, but rather to convey a more urgent sense of the interdependence between things. So vast and yet so detailed is imperialism as an experience with crucial cultural dimensions, that we must speak of overlapping territories, intertwined histories common to men and women, whites and non-whites, dwellers in the metropolis and on the peripheries, past as well as present and future; these territories and histories can only be seen from the perspective of the whole of secular human history.

NARRATIVES
OF NAVAJO-NESS
FOUR

Two prominent alteric strategies, both born of a counterhegemonic ideology that resists and challenges American domination, are being used to revitalize Navajo society and to define a dignified and favorable sense of what it is to be Navajo. The first is the use of alteric discourse (which, for the purposes of this discussion, is defined as "talk" and as oral or written narrative) to revitalize the image of Navajos by renegotiating and widely communicating a constellation of distinctive and "authentic" elements that make up a positive cultural and national Navajo identity. The second, discussed in the following chapter, is the transformation of institutions on the Navajo Reservation in ways that make them feel more Navajo. In examining how discourse plays a role in constituting this Navajo-ness, I focus on narratives about topics that Navajos at Diné College themselves highlight—history, culture, and language—as well as other subjects found in speeches and writings aimed at large public audiences. I also explore "talk" of the sort found in pair or small group conversations or interviews. The genres of discourse include Navajo biographical and autobiographical narratives, sacred and secular pedagogy, traditional oral history and origin "myths," and Western-style historical accounts.

Discourse (in its various facets) may be used as a problem-solving strategy in bringing about this desired Navajo cultural revitalization. An understanding of the ways in which the Navajo present is felt to be unsatisfactory requires a knowledge and an understanding of the past, as well as of Navajo traditional beliefs. According to traditional oral history, creation stories, and other teaching stories—such as Coyote stories—there was a time in the past when Navajos had received and were living according to the Blessing Way teachings of the Holy People. This was a time when animals talked and the Navajo people lived in balance and harmony with nature and with each other. Navajo narratives of these marvelous and mythic times can be told only in the winter months, but Navajos wishing to make an unfavorable comment about the present can refer to these stories and teachings at any time. This look at the past serves as a diagnostic tool; it allows people to compare the imperfect present with the past and to determine where the discrepancies lie.

Another aspect of this narrative-utilizing strategy is to apply the narrative to the present. For instance, Frank Morgan was discussing the problems that Navajos were having with their neighbors at the time. He said:

> When a problem comes up—people drive up to your car and vandalize it or they kill your dog or shoot your cattle or attack your brother and beat him up real bad. You're going to be really mad and want the ultimate punishment. What we say from the medicine man side, "We are SN [Sa'ąh Naagháí]." Adáhodíyin, having sacred respect for the self. Stop and say, "I'm SN, and I'm a particular kind of Holy People. My thought and words are going to be effective." You don't say, "That person is going to die!" The air that we breathe is the same as Talking God and Holy Wind People. That's what's inside us. We breathe it and speak by it. We are using the breath of the Holy Wind People for what we say. The thing that makes us talk and gives us our characteristic voice is lightning. So Sky has a voice. Earth has a voice. Wind, insects—all that is the voice of the earth. We're all the same. We have the same principle inside it. I have to be harmonious. BH [Bik'eh Hózhóón] principles because I don't want to get myself in trouble over what happened. (April 4, 1995)

Then, to extend the lesson to a situation immediately at hand in the college community, he continued, "Here's where we need to create an awareness. These administrators when they apply discipline need to apply principles, not shoot in the dark. Protection Way and Blessing Way principles. If we follow these, we won't have to fear. But we have administrators who are not trained administrators who don't know how to handle problems."

Another narrative component in this process is for people to describe their own experiences, or those of a relative or a well-known person, with a problem and how they dealt with it. These biographical and autobiographical narratives allow Navajos to transmit alteric, ideology-laden messages and to offer themselves as models of how to be truly Navajo. For instance, at the February 3, 1994, student assembly at Navajo Community College, Phil Bluehouse, president of the college's board of regents, provided the "welcome" to the assembly. After introducing himself in Navajo by naming his four clans, he gave a brief lecture about "traditional values" and the importance of knowing each other's clans. He then told about his struggle to get where he was that day. He talked about his hard work and about how he had to push himself. He said:

You hear me talk Navajo. I knew no English until I was fifteen. But years down the road, here I am. You are here as adults with grandchildren coming up. Young people have children and you have to do things either for yourself or for the young people. We'll see people talk nothing but English and we'll see people who are versatile, who can speak the language and eat the food, sheep's head, eat the eyes, the tongue. . . . If you've lost that, you'll have no traditional values or you will be different. You are here at NCC because that's part of the teaching, and hopefully that's what you will carry on. . . . I wrote fifteen pages of papers, but I left them in the truck and decided to speak from my heart. . . . regardless of difficulty and hardship. See them as challenges, all these that we call hardship. . . . Remember there was a man by the name of Bluehouse. That's the way I see those elders who have shared their thoughts with me.

In this speech, Bluehouse uses himself as an example of a Navajo who knows, and who has benefited from knowing, his culture. He's the real thing; he speaks his language, he has his traditional values, he eats the food. He is speaking to Navajo students who are facing many challenges and hardships as they grow up and become adults with responsibilities for children and grandchildren of their own, and he offers himself as a living testimony to Navajo-ness and its rewards.

Another component of discourse is its power to represent and reimagine the past in strategic ways. One source of this power is the way in which discourse (written and oral) allows displacement—of these representations of the past in time and space. We are familiar with the fact that until fairly recently, Indians have been treated solely from a Western perspective in American history. One aspect of that treatment has been the focus on "Indian wars"; earlier textbooks emphasized the "bloodthirsty savage" motif and represented Indians as aggressive and rapacious. Presently, these chapters are being rewritten to stress the defensive nature of many Indian military engagements with whites. In addition, events such as the four-year imprisonment of Navajos at Bosque Redondo are now accurately being labeled incarcerations in concentration camps rather than the more innocuous-sounding "relocations" or "resettlements." Discourse—whether historical narratives or labeling—has the power to reach back in time and space and change the way all of us remember and think about and are influenced by events in our collective past.

In addition to uncovering and naming relations of domination and aggression, the ability of discourse to re-represent the past also gives Navajos the means to use it creatively as a reference point for the renovation of contemporary conceptualizations of Navajo culture and tribal community. Authors of discourse inevitably present "facts" as well as clues to how these facts should be interpreted. This dual accomplishment is possible through skillful use of fictional devices; thus, the author selects certain facts and details from all those possible and plots them in such a way that a desired ideology, sentiment, or weight is also communicated and impressed upon the audience. This allows an author to privilege one version and to discredit or trivialize others. For example, when Navajos quite seriously say that they "won" World War II through the use of their unique language, they are making an important ideological point about their history of loyalty and their contributions to the United States and its other citizens. However, this point is made at the expense of many other individuals and groups who also had something to do with the allied forces' victory.

Another example of this desire of Navajos to control the ways in which they are defined and represented can be seen in the following words of Anthony Lee, Sr.:

> Not just say that, "On the reservation here we have a hogan, you know. And we have a sheep here, this, and we have a sheep. This is how you butcher a sheep. On the reservation, we have the beautiful canyons, like Canyon de Chelly, you know. On the reservation, the woman, they weave rugs, you know, beautiful rugs, and this is what they weave it on, the loom, you know. On the reservation, we have yucca plant, you know. Yucca plant is used in the ceremonies, you know." I think we need to break away from that cliches, you know, that stereotyping, you know. That's good for the tourists, but that's not good medicine for me, you know. It just literally turns me off the minute I start hearing people talk that way. "The Navajos, the Diné people came by way of the Bering Strait," you know, that sort of thing, you know. It's something wrong with that, you know; there's no life in it, you know. "The stoic Indian," you know, that totem pole that you see in front of the trading post of that Indian, you know, that "Me big chief" sit there, "Me big chief," you know. "Wow!" You know, the totem pole, that buying artifacts, you know. These kids that come from the east, they buy these headdress, you know, take it back and say, "Hey, I been to Indian country! I seen real Injuns and live Injuns," you know. (July 24, 1994)

In this passage, Lee first evokes, then rejects, the simplistic images that have frequently been used to pigeonhole and contain Navajos and other Native Americans. He asserts two things: that there is more to Indians than can be captured in these few features that make up the tourist's perception and that these narrow representations of Indians can be wrong and hurtful.

Beyond the issue of the actual content that is used in representing Navajos is the question of who has the right or the appropriate knowledge to use the contents of Navajos' own discourse. This is a controversial issue, one in which anthropologists are perennially implicated, and it made headlines in the tribal newspaper, the *Navajo Times*, following the 1997 annual Navajo Studies Conference. Sandra T. Francis, who is identified in the article as "an Anglo cultural anthropologist, registered nurse, and dancer interested in the power of healing," was challenged by members of the audience when she presented her research findings on "what occurs inside the hogan during the Nightway Ceremony and talked about movements of the Yei dancers." A portion of the Navajo Times article (Becenti 1997) reads:

> *Once the discussion was open to the public, Francis was hit with all sorts of commentary, including the belief that women should not talk about the ceremony, that such a discussion should not take place during the Spring season, and whether or not she had the license to write details of the sacred dance.*
>
> *"A person has to be properly initiated before he can talk or hear about the Yei Bei Chei," said Johnson Dennison, a medicineman and cultural specialist working with Navajo Community College, who explained to Francis and the mostly non-Indian audience why Navajo audience members raised concerns.*
>
> *"In the Navajo way, any discussion about sacred ceremonies, like Yei Bei Chei, is t'oo baa hasti' (it's sensitive). That sort of discussion can stay with you, raising the emotions inside of you," Dennison said. "The only way you can overcome it is with the help of a medicineman. Only a medicineman can undo that emotion. If one does not do that, it affects your body and your mind."*
>
> *Navajo audience members said even the most basic information should not be shared with any general audience. Eulinda Toledo Benally was among the group. She felt Francis crossed the boundaries.*
>
> *"What struck me is how she tried to justify her actions. She claimed that human beings are all alike and we should try to understand each other. If she really wanted to understand us, she would not have done this," said Toledo Benally, who believes it is time for more Navajo scholars and researchers to present their own topics. There were less than a handful of Navajos who read from their papers.*
>
> *"I felt the comments made about this topic were a blessing in disguise. Non-Navajos need to understand why this is so precious to us and why we are so protective of it. I strongly believe that before anyone researches or studies a topic, they should ask the tribal people themselves. Then, ask the people what is or is not appropriate to write or talk about," said Chenoa Bah Stilwell, who served as a moderator and is a member of the conference committee.*

The very fact that Navajos now challenge not only the content of what is being written about them but also the right of non-Navajos to research, write, and speak about their culture at all is a sign of resistance to the hegemonic society that had denied them a voice in their affairs and had, for a century or more, done all their talking for them. There is a growing resistance to non-Navajos' researching Navajo topics, particularly ceremonial ones.

Furthermore, the Western research mode appears inappropriate at best and offensive at worst to many Navajos. I was once told by Harry Walters that the object of telling the traditional stories is not so that they can be analyzed. He said, "The object of the stories is to understand your relationship to the natural world."

While the counterhegemonic ideology expressed by the challenge to the anthropologist's work on the ceremonials is itself noteworthy, another interesting facet of the comments on Francis's paper is the effort on the part of Stilwell and Benally to represent the Navajo perspective on such research as uniform. In fact, Francis had asked "tribal people" for access to the dances and information about their interpretation, and her requests had been granted. In a letter to the editor in the same issue of the newspaper, she explained that "with the permission of two Dine families, I was able to begin learning about the Nightway ceremony, particularly the dances. I was instructed by these families to follow the rules: no photography, no tape recording, and no questions about things that were too sacred to be shared. I followed these rules. The knowledge that was shared with me was to be used in two ways: to educate other Euro-Americans and to benefit The People in any way possible" (Francis 1997:A-4).

Yet another characteristic of discourse is its power to attach an authoritative interpretation or understanding to an event, object, person, or thing, even when the senses or experience of the audience would dictate a different interpretation. This is a very important point; well-crafted, effective discourse can cause us to deny the meaning of what we see or hear in favor of an account that pleases or lulls us. A perfectly obvious example of this is the fact that formal counterhegemonic discourse—in the form of politicians' speeches, graduation addresses, newspaper articles about Navajo language fairs, and so on—has convinced many Navajo people that schools on the Navajo Reservation are generally successful in transmitting and maintaining the Navajo language despite the massive evidence of their own eyes and ears in their own homes and communities that this is not the case. Joshua Fishman (1991:89) has cautioned about just this sort of thing, stating that "no amount of lectures in Xish [his term for the indigenous language in question], theater performances in Xish, Xish song recitals, books or journals in Xish, prizes and award ceremonies for Xish authors, . . . nor even endless rounds of 'intergeneration visiting' . . . can substitute for the re-establishment of young families of child-bearing age in which Xish is the normal medium or co-medium of communication and/or of other culturally appropriate home, family, neighborhood and community intergenerational vernacular activity."

All of these characteristics of discourse make it effective for challenging a hegemonic perspective (on historical events, figures, or encounters, for instance), crafting a counterhegemonic alternative, and then disseminating it. When these counterhegemonic objectives are carried out through discursive strategies, hegemony is challenged and engaged on its own ground; discourse won these hegemonic goals in the first place via propagandistic newspaper accounts, media offerings (movies, fiction, art), textbooks, scholarly publications, documentaries, business reports, religious tracts, and government publications. Navajos are using their own discourse to challenge that hegemony. The subordination, denigration, commercial exploitation, commodification, and trivialization of Native Americans, including Navajos, were and continue to be accomplished through discourse.

As a means to resist these efforts to erase them from serious consideration as human beings in all their complexity, Navajos employ alteric strategies to assert that they are the opposite of what has been said about them. They say, "We are the children of the Holy People." They say that the Diné were created as part of beautiful nature and still have a home there. Harry Walters explained the comfort, the security, the belonging that are gifts of a Navajo identity: "In Navajo it is said that there are twelve places where you are loved, where you are cared for. So therefore never have the attitude that nobody cares. Never say, 'This is my life; I can do anything I want to with it. It's none of your business.' This is not the attitude to have. There are places, like the lakes, streams, the mountain where the first sunlight hits, the beautiful birds sing. These places like this, this is where you are cared for and where you are thought of as a child. You are their child, their baby; that's what it is. So I think that's a good attitude to have" (October 7, 1994).

In public events, many beautiful stories of Navajo-ness are told. Every event, every public occasion is marked repeatedly by narratives and other performances that signal that this is a very Navajo event that is taking place. At Diné College, speakers introduce themselves by their clans in the Navajo language. The occasion is begun with an invocation, often performed in Navajo and sometimes by a medicine man. The various speakers exhort the audience over and over about the importance of the Navajo language and culture to Navajo people. In the general assembly mentioned earlier, Phil Bluehouse spoke about the clan system and traditional Navajo foods. He was followed by Guy Gorman, a respected Navajo elder who was one of the founders of Navajo Community College as well as one of the famous code talkers. Gorman exhorted the audience to learn and maintain their Navajo ways. He said, "We should all know the history and traditional values of the

Navajo tribe. We talk Navajo and that's our language. . . . We want to possess that language. The Navajo Nation has its own government, sovereignty and money. . . . We need language and tradition. Be proud of what you are. This needs to be taught to our Navajo kids coming up."

Tommy Lewis, then president of Diné College, spoke at a similar event in September 1994. In his speech, he used the word *k'é*, which Benjamin Barney (July 11, 1997) identified as a philosophical religious concept that defines for Navajos their relationships—including concomitant attitudes and behaviors—not only with family and clan members but also with their environment and lifestyle. Lewis began his message to the students by telling them about the college they were attending:

> *Our forefathers did the right thing to have a college of our own. It's best for students to stay on the reservation for college. It's a wonderful gesture they made. We're taking advantage of the opportunity, you as students, and us as employees. Our educational philosophy is different. It's built on our own teaching philosophy. . . . The college is here for you. . . . How can we prepare students? We want traditional Navajo traditions plus modern things. . . . We want a connection and culture and also conform to the standards . . . of any other college. This has to do with what you want. In the past, someone else was taking care of you. Your parents, mothers and fathers, did that for you. They continue to do it; it's a natural part of being a parent. Some want to take rein and plan their own life the way your grandmother and elders taught you. We can't deviate from these teachings at NCC. . . . K'é, that's what makes it all happen. It's a word in Navajo. . . . I'm sure a lot of you are enrolled within your culture—Navajo language, Navajo culture. . . . We start practicing it here, if you don't already know it.*

This narrative conveys a strong alteric message about the differentness that students can expect at Diné College. "This is a Navajo institution; it's for Navajo students; it's based on Navajo principles; we practice Navajo language and culture here."

Lewis's message was echoed by the next speaker, Paul Willeto, then dean of instruction, who first introduced himself in Navajo and then repeated his clans in English. He summed up and reinforced the points made before him: "Sa'ąh Naagháí Bik'eh Hózhóón is a philosophy we're proud of. We try to incorporate Navajo teachings into the curriculum. Our goal as an institution is to do this. This is one of our strengths and we're proud of it. . . . Now there's the culture and language program. It's Navajo Nation wide. There is a lot of demand for it in the community.

Here at the college we require nine hours in Navajo and Indian Studies. This is a Navajo institution and it's important to instill this in future generations."

Can there be any doubt that this institution means business about supporting the Navajo language, culture, and overall identity? The flood of talk about Navajo-ness, the content that defines and defines again what this college is, the performances of Navajo-ness, the Navajo faces and Navajo voices—there would appear to be nothing to contradict or question the absolute truth of these assertions. This is the power of discourse to represent reality—if, in fact, what is being represented as real is real. But most importantly, this is the power of discourse to make what is not yet real into something that will one day be real. And part of this power of discourse is that an audience does not know the difference. Is what they have just heard really real? Or is it speech that is working ritually to make what they have just heard into reality?

The role that discourse—talk or narrative—plays in the future of the Navajo language is tied to the points made above. The discourse—the "narratives of Navajo-ness"—that I am describing and illustrating does its very best to represent and to construct a counterhegemonic ideology that celebrates otherness, a Navajo-ness that is the opposite of anything Western. This totalizing discourse can be recognized as a problem-solving strategy, a tool or maybe a weapon in building a new reality for Navajos, a revitalized, distinctive, and authentic Navajo-ness. The problem for the Navajo people, however, is the same as that for the audiences being addressed by the speakers I have quoted. Does the discourse represent the really real or the wished-for real? If the Navajo people cannot tell or are unwilling or reluctant to tell the difference, then they, their language, and their culture may be in jeopardy. If the discourse truly represents something real, then effective steps are indeed being taken to maintain and transmit the traditional heritage of the Navajos—language, culture, and identity. If the discourse is merely representing the wished-for real, then the Navajo people ought to be vigilant; they might want to look and listen about them for the evidence of their eyes and ears. Are children speaking the Navajo language? Are they seeing materials, other than token labels and signs, written in Navajo? Are they and their family and clan members using and teaching the language and culture?

The possibility that there is a contrast between the health and vitality of the Navajo language as represented in the public discourse I have described and what may be observed by speakers on the ground is a crucial issue. The evidence of my eyes and ears tells me that there is often a wide and deep chasm between individuals' statements about the necessity or inevitability of Navajos' knowing and using their tribal language and their actual language practices. I attribute this to ideological conflict—people know the discourse (what they should say) and they often say it, especially in public situations. Perhaps they also know what they and others should do (use and teach the language to the youth) if the language is to live on; right now, a great number of people are not doing it. There are a number of reasons why that is so.

Some people say they do not have the time or the knowledge. Others were never taught when they were growing up. Pauline Manygoats (pseudonym) finds herself in that position: "Because some parents, we really don't know all of the stuff. Because our parents really never taught us all those stuff. They'll say, 'It has to be holy,' you know. 'It has to be this way. You have to be this way'" (February 5, 1995).

Others recognize that the schools, for a variety of reasons, are not as effective as they would like them to be in teaching the language in a way that will result in its transmission from generation to generation. They see a gap between the degree of language proficiency that many expect from the schools and what the schools are actually able to deliver. Della Toadlena explained: "Right now, Navajo language, I think, is taught to a few select groups at NCC. And these people, I don't think go and really do anything with it. Just a few college students learn it. And then, they don't do anything else with it. I don't know. It has to be taught some other way differently than the way it's being done right now, in order for children to learn it, to learn to speak it again. . . . 'Cause at school, I think you can only do so much." She continued: "Although we have schools where, you know, I don't think it really teaches them to learn Navajo, though, 'cause I have a niece that's taking Navajo language, and she doesn't know, she doesn't speak Navajo, so she has to take it. But it's not teaching her anything. It tells her to say, 'Clouds, or white clouds, are in the sky.' I mean, after she says that, so what? you know. That's not teaching her to speak it" (September 27, 1995).

Barbara Singer (pseudonym) also had concerns about the degree of proficiency her children are acquiring in their Navajo language classes. On one hand, she said, "But, you know, they're learning, like at school, we have the language teachers, the Navajo language teachers." On the other hand, she feared that this was inadequate. "Yes, I think [the Navajo language] should be taught more. 'Cause I think in where, well, my daughter, she was in third grade, and I think the language and culture teacher came around like once a week, for an hour. And that's not enough. It needs to be more than that, every day, so many hours a day" (July 27, 1995).

In some cases, children do not know their Navajo language because for some parents, Navajo language is not an educational priority. Other times, parents are deciding not to teach their children the Navajo language. Della Toadlena had observed this; she explained: "A lot of people don't want their children to learn Navajo and so they're not teaching it to them. I can see it in my own brothers and sisters where one brother has five children. They don't speak Navajo at all. A sister has four children; they know a little, a little of Navajo and they can't speak it; they can understand it a little bit. When somebody gives them a command, they can do it. But otherwise, they can't speak it. So, no, I think more and more kids are not learning Navajo."

Celeste Charley (pseudonym) had seen this in her own family: "I have cousins . . . that can't speak Navajo. They're full-blooded Navajo and you wonder, there must have been a time, and I know it was there because I've heard it before, where parents they decided not to teach their kids Navajo because they didn't want them to be unsuccessful or they wanted . . . them to be more successful or more fluent in English and that same idea I guess from early age has been forced on them that you got to learn it this way and this is the only way and you can't be thinking about your other way, otherwise . . . it's going to hold you back, kind of idea" (June 1, 1994).

Yet other parents say that they will teach their children the language later, after the children have mastered English and other academic subjects. I have close friends who get annoyed at the pressure from Navajo language educators around them who criticize and blame them for not passing the language on to their children. They say they'll decide what's best for their children and it's no one's business but their own.

There is also a traditional teaching that I have heard spoken of several times that says that the language will take care of itself. Anthony Lee, Sr., spoke of this teaching when I interviewed him: "So I guess we could say that there's a built in safety mechanism; language protects itself. No matter what, even the Japanese people have not figured out still what that secret code was. They still have not figured even though it was made public. It was held a secret a long time. Now they think they know it, but there's this secrecy. It stays that way. We got no control over it. That's what I'm talking about" (July 28, 1994).

Some Navajos are relatively complacent because there are still so many speakers that they feel the language can never die. Others know that they themselves and members of their own family speak it, and they may assume that they are representative of the Navajo people as a whole. Benjamin Barney, for example, truly does practice what he describes in the following passage; I have often seen and heard him prompt those around him—at work, in restaurants and stores, wherever he goes—to speak Navajo. If he were the norm, advocates of the Navajo language would have nothing to worry about. The question is, how many other Navajos share his degree of commitment? He says,

If I look at Paul Platero's study and say most of the younger kids are not speaking as well or not understanding Navajo, more and more of them are doing that. And more and more of their days and their weeks and months are done in English, then yet, I say, "Whoa! You know, something needs to be done." But when on the other side, I look at myself and I am not about to clunk over next week or month or two years. I will retain my spoken Navajo. And I will still enforce it on all my relatives and I will enforce it on people in my work and many places, I think, more and more. And as I'm doing that, it's going, and I intend to be around for awhile, you know, like thirty years, forty years. So the spoken Navajo will still be there thirty, forty years, I think. . . . It's not going to really die. Part of that is not really realistic. There are people, places where we only speak Navajo. There are people where my total communication with them is only Navajo. And I don't think that that's going to stop in the next ten years. I think it'll still be there twenty years, thirty years down the road, that I will continue to speak Navajo to these people. And there are many other Navajos that are like me, I think, that are in that situation and we just clearly need to recognize that. . . . And I tend to speak Navajo at trading posts, at gas stations. And I cannot pray, there's no way I can pray in English. I can't; it's just next to impossible to do that. There are parts of me and things that I do that I cannot switch over to English. And this is true, I think, for many. Many Navajos will not pray in English, even if they're bilingual. It's just something that's really hard to do. (September 1, 1994)

Several people reported that it was not uncommon for Navajo children to refuse to learn or use the language, and their parents could do nothing about it. Alfred James, who has worked as a custodian at Diné College, said, "If you talk Navajo, you know, if you talk Navajo, you can [teach it to your kids], but they don't want to listen. They want the jazz and all that music. They listen there" (July 28, 1994).

Are these situations and reasons mighty enough to make it unlikely that Navajos will maintain their language? There are additional circumstances that contribute to a pessimistic picture. Although the teachings and the language are still present in Navajo life, still accessible through middle-aged and elderly Navajos, there are great difficulties in making them available and meaningful to the younger generations of Navajos. My students have told me that there are many people (particularly the elderly) who do not want to talk to the youth, who criticize and condemn their less than fluent performances in the Navajo language and who push them away because they don't measure up to past standards of Navajo-ness. Perhaps these individuals do not see the urgency because the presence of language and culture is something they take for granted; it has always been there, and they were taught that it always would be. Perhaps it is as Fishman (1996) said: the elders take pride in belonging to an exclusive club—the last really fluent speakers of an old and less changed variety of their native language. Whatever the reason, the very individuals who are the best speakers of the language are, more often than one would think, the least willing to tolerate or cooperate with young Navajo students of the language.

Benjamin Barney, director of the Diné Teacher Education Program at Diné College.

The Ned A. Hatathli Center (opposite, top), the Culture Center on the Tsaile campus of Diné College. Its shape was inspired by Tsaile Peak (opposite, bottom), and it was modeled on a traditional Navajo log hogan, like the one shown above, which is maintained on the Tsaile campus of Diné College for the ceremonial use of staff and students.

Harry Walters, director of the Ned Hatathli Museum and the Center for Diné Studies at Diné College.

Wilson Aronilth (left), a Diné College instructor and medicine man, stands with Donald Denetdeal, a history instructor and Blessing Way singer, in front of a mural depicting the Navajo Emergence myth.

NAVAJO-IZATION
OF NAVAJO SCHOOLS

FIVE

For many Navajos, it is a source of pride and honor that they belong to a Native American tribe; it gives them a distinctive and special identity. Likewise, it is important to them that the Navajo Nation is a sovereign nation—a nation within a nation. Yet because their Navajo Nation continues to be subjugated and exploited by the larger and more powerful United States, they experience a conflict and uneasiness with their dual nationality. To cope with this unpleasant feeling, they are taking active steps to address the situation.

One potentially powerful antidote to this sense of being under the control of the United States involves transforming the social institutions on the Navajo Reservation—Navajo-izing them into ones that feel more reflective of Navajo culture and more responsive to Navajo problems and needs. This transformation involves mitigating or masking the obvious Western origins, functions, and operations of these state and civil institutions—schools, churches and other religious entities, social services, even the tribal government—on the Navajo Reservation. The work that is done to obscure the Western elements and make them appear as Navajo as possible is accomplished in many ways—some superficial and trivial, some highly symbolic and satisfying, and some fairly substantive. One of the most Navajo-ized of all Navajo Nation institutions is the school.

A BRIEF POLITICAL
HISTORY OF NAVAJO
EDUCATION

It was not until after they returned from their Long Walk to Fort Sumner (Hwééldi) that the Navajos were introduced to formal American education. The Treaty of 1868, which set the terms of the peace between the Navajos and the United States military, contained an Article VI, which concluded with a provision that the federal government would provide for the education of Navajo children. This article, found in Appendix H of Bill Acrey's *Navajo History: The Land and the People* (1979:321), reads:

> *In order to insure the civilization of the Indians entering into this treaty, the necessity of education is admitted, especially of such of them as may be settled on said agricultural parts of this reservation, and they therefore pledge themselves to compel their children, male and female, between the ages of six and sixteen years, to attend school; and it is hereby made the duty of the agent for said Indians to see that this stipulation is strictly complied with; and the United States agrees that, for every thirty children between said ages who can be induced or compelled to attend school, a house shall be provided, and a teacher competent to teach the elementary branches of an English education shall be furnished, who will reside among said Indians, and faithfully discharge his or her duties as a teacher.*

From their first exposure to Western schooling, Navajos had mixed feelings. Some perceived schools as the ladder on which Navajo youths would climb to success. This was expressed in the now-famous words of Chief Manuelito, one of the most powerful and respected Navajo headmen of the early American conquest period. His experiences with the American military and other Anglos who were exerting increasing control over Navajo affairs led him to see certain advantages to formal education. He is reported to have said, "My grandchild, the whites have many things we Navajos need but cannot get. It is as though the whites were in a grassy valley, with wagons, plows, and plenty of food, we Navajos up on a dry mesa. We can hear them talking, but we cannot get to them. My grandchild, school is the ladder. Tell our people this" (Link 1968:55, quoted in Acrey 1979:124).

Others felt that schools and their subject matter were evils necessary for survival. King Mike, an instructor at Diné College, described his father's beliefs about the preparation his children would need for their futures: "And he said, 'I'm going to raise my five kids differently.' And so he said, 'You don't need to learn Navajo. You don't have to know the ceremonies. All you have to know is how to read and write English, 'cause that's what's coming.' He said, 'Navajos, they're going to be gone'" (September 26, 1994).

There were also some children who wanted badly to go to school but were kept away by their parents or grandparents, who felt that the schools had nothing to contribute to the lives of Navajo people. Max Hanley (1977:30) was one of these children. When, in 1916, he brought up the subject of going to school, his grandfather responded, "Oh, no! What are you saying, my grandson? People like you are not put in school. It's only for those who don't have homes and just roam around, the ones who are not well-mannered—they are the ones who are put in school. What would you do over there? You have livestock here—sheep that we depend on, wool that we depend on. We sell the lambs in the fall; we eat mutton; and if you go to school who's going to feed you mutton? So what you are thinking is useless."

There has been a variety of schools on the Navajo Reservation over time, but most of the early ones were boarding schools, and these are the ones most discussed by Navajos even now. For many Navajos, boarding schools are synonymous with the coercive and belittling treatment they have received at the hands of the dominant society. It is interesting that even teenage students who have never attended boarding schools can retell their relatives' stories of those times and feel the indignities as if they were fresh and firsthand.

The Indian boarding schools were modeled on the pioneering efforts of General Richard Henry Pratt at his Carlisle Indian School, founded in Pennsylvania in 1878. Pratt believed that the role of education was to wean the Indian from his native traditions and replace them with the "civilizing" influences of white American culture. He strongly favored the total assimilation of the American Indian into the dominant culture, and he felt that the best and most efficient way to do this was to take Indian children away from their families and culture and immerse them in the language and culture of middle-class American society.

In the 1920s, it was discovered that only a small fraction of school-age Navajo children were attending school. Because the Navajo population was scattered over the vast reservation, where roads were unpaved and frequently impassable and where transportation was inadequate, the Bureau of Indian Affairs of the Department of the Interior decided that the only practical solution was for the children to attend boarding schools modeled on Pratt's "successful" example. To provide these boarding schools with students, parents were compelled to allow their children to attend. Paul Blatchford (1977:178) said, "The police forced those kids to go to school, and I knew many parents whose teardrops fell—but they couldn't do anything about it. If the parents resisted the policemen, they were put in jail; so there was really nothing they could do."

When Gloria Emerson (1983:659) wrote that these and more recent boarding schools "have been educating Navajo children to become 'biological Navajos' without knowing their tribal history, culture, language, or land," she was referring to the fact that the function of schools is to reproduce the social order of the state that builds and supports them. In Western society, schools play the most powerful role—after the home and family—in the socialization of children. It is at school that young people learn about the social institutions that make up their society and the roles and statuses that are available to them. As John Macionis (1994:62) explained it: "Schools initially teach basic skills such as reading, writing, and arithmetic, and later offer advanced knowledge that students will need to assume a specialized role in their complex society. Beyond formal lessons, however, the school's so-called *hidden curriculum* imparts important cultural values." Among the values of American schools are those that favor competition over cooperation, that communicate beliefs about the worth of one culture compared with another, that define appropriate gender roles, and so on. These sanctioned practices are those through which the hegemony is reproduced and reinforced. Elizabeth Mertz (1992:325–326) noted that research in classroom settings has frequently found in the language of the classroom "a powerful orienting social practice." She continued: "Hidden behind the apparent content of a lesson may be a deeper message about how the world operates, about what kind of knowledge counts, about who may speak and how to proceed—a cultural worldview that is quietly conveyed through classroom language. Thus we can see broader social patterns and struggles played out and transformed in the smaller-scale dynamics of classroom education."

Over the years, periods of awareness of the coercive and destructive aspects of Western schooling on the Navajo people alternated with periods of educational reform and cultural sensitivity. Anita Pfeiffer (1996), a prominent Navajo educator and former director of the Navajo Department of Education, described her experiences in the 1940s and 1950s. She thought it was "wonderful" that anthropologists such as Gladys Reichard taught the Navajo language in reservation schools and that Navajo language books were being produced for use in the schools. Although these innovations were seen as positive and were received gratefully by individual Navajos, school curriculum and policy decisions at this time were still in the hands of a succession of Anglo federal officials and administrators.

The 1950s saw a resurgence of boarding schools, especially for older students. Parents were usually strongly opposed to sending their small children away from home, but many felt it was a necessary sacrifice for the sake of the child and the tribe as a whole (Thompson 1975:118). Many of the stories that Navajos tell about their experiences illustrate the total lack of control they and their parents had concerning the process. Harry Walters described what he and his brothers and sisters went through when they first went to the Shiprock Boarding School.

> I went to school in the early fifties, right after the Navajo-Hopi Rehabilitation
> Act was passed in 1950. And so that act was the time where I call that period
> "the Great Leap Forward," you know. And to where a lot of schools were
> built and hospitals, you know. The NCC and buildings that we're occupying in
> Shiprock were built at that time. And then so only twenty percent of the Navajo
> and Hopi population were literate. And then so, a lot of children, you know,
> went to school at that time. My older brothers and sisters that were older than

me did not go to school. It was not the thing to do at that time. You know, nobody thought about going to school. But then there was a push by the tribal council and the agency; they went around enrolling children. So my younger brother, who was six years old, and I was seven, and my oldest sister who was about nine and my older brother who was about thirteen, we, our parents put us in the boarding school, the Shiprock Boarding School. It was a terrifying experience really, those first few days. And there were some older students; real old, you know, that were going to school there. And were all put in the same buildings and it was terrible and some of these students were urban. They lived in the Shiprock community, so they could speak a little bit of English. But most of us were from the sticks and some of us, that was probably the first time we ever used the indoor toilet and things like that. And the food was strange to us. So and then we hear English being spoken all the time, you know, and everything. It was very strange and terrifying to me. And I remember my younger brother was crying all the time and I had to comfort him. And then, at night, you know, each one of us had beds in different sec-tions. They divided us, you know, by age. My older brother went with the older students, so I was with my younger brother. We were in the section together. And then at night, you know, after everybody goes to sleep, I would go over there and crawl in bed with him and try to comfort him and go to sleep like that. And so, it was that kind of experience. (October 7, 1994)

Benjamin Barney explained that not only were there strange and frightening encounters with the Anglo school personnel and the unfamiliar physical setting, but Navajo children were also exposed to Navajos from other clan families and cultural traditions that were likewise foreign and unsettling:

But when I got there, we had to do a lot of changes. Our clothes had to be changed. The kinds of buildings that we lived in, just everything. And meeting for the first time white Americans. I mean we were secluded from that. We didn't mix. Even meeting a lot of the kids from other clan families, that was enough of a culture foreignness for me. So it was a totally different experience. It wasn't only that there were non-Navajos, but just the whole system of the dormitory BIA school. The teachers that are white people that we were told are way on the other side of any reasonableness than anything. They were there. And then we, on top of that is just kids from other families that we were not used to. And our ways within the clan family was quite different from that. But there was this really strong enforcement of how the school is to run. And it didn't really consider differences between families that we had to adjust to. (September 1, 1994)

Della Toadlena remembered being so excited about the prospect of beginning her education that she was crying, "I want to go to school! I want to go to school!" She was struck, however, by some of the inexplicable behaviors of the Anglos in these strange places:

Oh, my goodness, let's see. The things that stand out vividly in my mind was having to take a tablespoon full of cod liver oil and I didn't particularly look forward to that. . . . And then I remember also when I first arrived at school, her marking in huge black letters all my clothes with the number 37, you know. They didn't care if it ran everywhere, but that's what happened. So we had great big numbers of our shirts and pants and so forth. . . . And I remember being herded around like animals into the showers.

My mother was all flustered. I couldn't imagine what the problem was. I needed a name to go to school and I didn't have any. My parents were both not formally educated and everybody in the camp also had never been to school and they didn't know. I didn't understand what was wrong with my Indian name, you know. "Why can't we just use that? You know, I have a name." But no, my mother wouldn't have it. She said I had to have an English name. It just so happened, also, my uncle came and saved the day. He had been to the service and had been to school earlier. He said, "Call her Della."

I don't know where in the world he came up with Della. It could have been the name of a girlfriend or whatever, but I've been Della ever since. (September 27, 1994)

Paul Willeto initially attended boarding school not so much because of the educational advantages as out of necessity, so that his mother would not have to worry about his physical well-being. He commented, "I guess what I'm trying to say is, because we were poor and it was difficult for my mother to [take care of us without my father], she even said that to me at one time, you know, 'Life is pretty hard. If you go to school, boarding school, they give you three meals a day. You have a good place to sleep, you know; you have a bed and all that stuff.' And that was really one of the reasons why she sent me to Crownpoint Boarding School along with my sister and some of my older brothers" (May 22, 1994).

Whatever the reasons students and their parents had for their decisions, there is no denying the very negative aspects of these institutions in regard to the cultural and linguistic identities of the children who attended. Ben Barney was clear in his indictment of the system: "I think it was outright really abusing students, wiping away another culture, another language. . . . It was very clear our language, our religion, our custom, was not something that we should practice or carry on with."

Ferlin Clark echoed this criticism and described the emotional impact of these policies on him and his classmates: "I think then a lot of the boarding school methods of teaching kids were done in a very unempowering way. They discouraged you so much that sometimes we would run away from the classroom. It was always, they were breaking your spirit" (February 6, 1995).

This attack on the very core of Navajo identity among vulnerable Navajo children can be recognized as hegemonic domination of the most heinous sort. As Gloria Anzaldúa (1987:59) wrote, "So, if you want to really hurt me, talk badly about my language. Ethnic identity is twin skin to linguistic identity—I am my language. Until I can take pride in my language, I cannot take pride in myself." It was a cold-blooded attempt to destroy the Navajos as a distinct people—under the guise of paternalistic efforts to "civilize" and even "save" them.

One of the damaging aspects of the schools was the degree to which they indoctrinated Navajos themselves to carry out the government's cultural and linguistic policies. Frank Morgan spoke about the anguish he felt when his basic beliefs and values were attacked:

When I was very little, some of the very harshest disciplinarians were not non-Indians. The harshest disciplinarians were Navajo women in the BIA school system there. . . . And then there was some, especially the Navajo personnel, were really against a lot of things that the background that I came from, the environment that I came from, culture and—not so much language, you know, at first, but they were saying to learn the Anglo way of life. That was what was going to save us. That now you have to leave your life, the way you lived it, and now you are in the Anglo way of life and you have to forget this other stuff, that it's all backwards. We shouldn't even think about it, you know. This other way is better and it makes more sense and so forth. This was the kind of propaganda coming from the Navajo personnel. . . . I was torn. And because it was kind of like tearing away who you were and what you really grew up with, and at that time I was very little, it caused me quite a bit of psychological problems. (August 29, 1994)

This assimilative brainwashing extended to religious instruction and indoctrination, which was an intrinsic part of BIA and Anglo education. New students were routinely asked which church they belonged to. Some students named denominations they had heard of or that family members belonged to. Students who stated no preference were assigned to a church, which they then were required to attend regularly. Wilson Aronilth, a Navajo culture instructor at Diné College, described his experiences with church-going during his school years:

It would be like, after the peace treaty of 1868, they said if you go to school,
you have to choose a church. In my time, we used to get a box of pieces of
paper and had to draw the name of a church. . . . What I learned, the earlier
part, when I was sent to a mission school, then they had the drawing at the BIA
school. I had to go to church every Sunday. . . . I drew Catholic, so I went
to Catholic church and learned a little about it—what to do and why they do
what they do. . . . Later, I drew Protestant and kept doing that. Then, it was
Mormon, then Nazarene. Each has a different philosophy. Some churches are
against other churches. I thought all religions were one, but it's not like that.
I came back and my grandfather who was a Blessing Way—Protection Way
singer questioned me. (August 29, 1994)

The general intent of this religious training was to erase the students' traditional religious beliefs and replace them with Christianity. The brutality of this practice can be clearly seen in the following description by Frank Morgan:

But what really got me was when the Navajo minister came on, he was very,
very harsh. He denounced and he renounced the Navajo way, the Navajo belief
systems. He said, "That's evil." And that, "If you ever think about those things,
if you ever do those things, you're going to a place that is burning down
below." And that, "God," you know, "that the good place up there, you're
never going to get there. You're going to go that way [pointing down]." . . . It
really affected you. I mean, they were horrible people. So they made you kind
of associate your medicine men and your leaders and whoever the influential
people are, that talked about Navajo culture ways, you know, you associated
with that and so, by that time, I was scared. I didn't know which way I was
going to go, what was going to happen to me. So I was going out of my mind
and I didn't resolve that until I was out of high school. So they really tore me
up, I guess. (August 29, 1994)

Several people attributed the current decline of the Navajo language and the
shame and stigma attached to a Navajo identity to the painful and demoralizing
experiences they or their older relatives had with language restrictions in their
youth. Renae Walters described her feelings on the subject:

I just feel that the United States government tried to take it [the Navajo
language] away from us. They almost succeeded; you see people who are
ashamed of who they are and I'd like to think that it's part of the United States'
fault, that because of them we're this way, that we're in this situation today.
It's because of them; they abused us; they made our ancestors walk on the
Long Walk. They made the older people not want to talk Navajo. . . . I'm glad

to live in this country, but I feel mad at them because they took away from us—any Native American—they took our, a lot of people's language. Some people, they don't even know their language. . . . They wish they knew, but they can't find it. They don't know it. And that what they did to us. And sometimes I feel mad about that. (April 24, 1995)

Frank Morgan elaborated: "There's quite a bit of shame and so forth. I think it has to do a lot with acculturation of the parents and grandparents in the contemporary society from the way things were done in the forties and fifties. And so there's been a lot of Westernization, a lot of shift away from the culture and language and that a lot of people are thinking that in their minds that Navajo culture and language is not the answer to successful survival, today and in their future."

This experience has been echoed by members of other tribes. Anna Lee Walters, a well-known author and an instructor at Diné College, is Pawnee-Otoe and married to a Navajo. In an earlier work (House and Reyhner 1996:144), I quoted her as saying, "There are three reasons for the breakdown of Otoe language: They were forced to leave their homeland and that affected language. There was a psychological factor, an emotional response to the loss. People became unwilling to learn the Otoe language because it was associated with pain and hurt. Older people speak about it in this way. There are only a few people left and everyone is related; therefore, people have to marry outside the tribe. There are only a few Otoes married to each other. In a mixed tribal marriage, family members use English."

For some, however, a painful language experience in school and elsewhere provided the motive for a "fight-back." As Simon Ortiz (1993:34–35) wrote: "I remembered my grandparents' and parents' words: educate yourself in order to help your people. In that era and the generation who had the same experience I had, there was an unspoken vow: we were caught in a system inexorably, and we had to learn that system well in order to fight back. Without the motive of a fight-back we would not be able to survive as the people our heritage had lovingly bequeathed us."

Some Navajos caught in the toils of boarding schools had that "fight-back" motivation and were able to resist the pressures against their language and culture. Renae Walters described the experience of her mother, who went to school during this era: "If they [students] talked their own language, they would wash their mouths out with soap, and nowadays I see a lot of people that don't talk Navajo. They're ashamed. But my mom, she always told me, 'They never whipped it out of me and they could never, no matter how much they washed my mouth out with soap, they would never take my language away from me and I could never feel ashamed of who I am because that's just me.'"

Benjamin Barney described his feelings about those boarding school pressures: "I never saw the language issue as positive. I always thought that the whole,
all those years, I don't think I can ever see it as positive—that my language, my culture, my religion, and my people were outlawed."

The Navajo discourse that continues to critique these and present-day Western
schools is clear. Western-style schools cannot meet Navajo needs because Navajos
have a different language, a different culture, a different sense of family, a different
religious and value system. There is also a strong belief that without these distinctive elements, a Navajo is seriously impaired when it comes to living his life and
facing the challenges ahead. Alvina Tsosie referred to this when she said:

> I would like to add something personal. I used to think that Anglo ways were
> somewhat better than Navajo ways. As a top student, I used to think that I
> would be happy learning more Anglo things than Navajo and get farther with
> only Anglo ways. I now know that I was very wrong. I realize now that without
> my culture and language, I would be nothing. Even if I had a doctorate degree
> and didn't know my culture, language, and especially my clan, that degree
> wouldn't mean anything. Even if I made a lot of money, that wouldn't mean
> anything either. I do plan to get a doctorate degree in whatever field I choose,
> but I will never forget who I am because I'm a Diné and I know my language,
> clan, and culture. I'm still learning about my culture every day and plan to
> never stop learning—both ways. I know I will be happy because I know who I
> am and where my people and I came from. I will pass this on to my children
> and grandchildren in the future. (October 4, 1994)

Despite the many negative aspects of these early (and not so early) boarding
schools and the opposition of some family members to them, many Navajos saw
them as having some positive and even essential features. The positive features of
boarding and other Western-style schools of the past that were named by a number
of the middle-aged people I interviewed, as well as by others of that generation,
included the discipline, hard work, and responsibility that were required of students; the respect that students were made to show for their teachers; the high
academic standards that were set for students; the love of learning that was incul-
cated in students; and the introduction the schools offered to the broader world.
In addition, a number of these people discussed their pleasure at being away from
the even stricter discipline and harder work of their family and community life. They
described the excitement of meeting new people and making new friends (especially from other tribes) and having opportunities to travel and experience new
things.

David Wallace Adams (1995:257, 260) described some of these positive attitudes as originating in a sort of pragmatism: "Some pessimistically concluded that the options facing Indians were exactly as policy makers defined them—assimilation or extinction. . . . by this line of reasoning, education was essential, not because it facilitated one's climb up the ladder of civilization, but because it ensured racial survival." Another pragmatic rationale he identified was the idea that education was "an essential weapon in the next generation's defense of tribal interests." He continued, "A final version of the pragmatic response can be seen in those students who chose school as a temporary escape from conditions at home. Poor food and clothing, an unhappy family situation, . . . the diminished expectations of reservation life, and even the oppressiveness of tribal tradition could induce children to prefer school over camp life."

However, another item can be added to this list of positive associations with boarding schools of the past: a certain attraction to and approbation of elements of Western society, a certain pull toward what is represented in some ways as a superior Western system. In his discussion of the accommodation that some Indian students and their parents made to the notion of Western schooling, Adams (1995) provided some chilling quotations from tribal members who had been converted to a belief in the superiority of all things Anglo. These people are quoted as saying things such as this lament by one Lakota boy away at school: "The progress of the Indian is not so rapid as it ought to be, but we cannot expect a whole race to reach the topmost round of civilization in a single generation" (Adams 1995:256). A Carlisle student, explaining to his mother why he would not be returning home from school the coming summer, said, "I expect, mother, you are looking for me to come home this summer, and no doubt you look toward the north where the hill is and wonder if I will come home over it as I used to when I came home from school when I was with you. Remember that I am here to learn still better way of the civilized people" (Adams 1995:257).

THE SELF-DETERMINATION MOVEMENT IN NAVAJO EDUCATION

The 1960s saw a national trend toward recognition and appreciation of ethnic groups in the United States, as well as an acknowledgment that they had been denied their civil rights and subjected to a great deal of unequal treatment, especially in the Eurocentric schooling that had been provided by the federal government. This was made particularly clear in 1969 in the report of the U.S. Senate's Special Subcommittee on Indian Education, chaired first by Senator Robert Kennedy and after his death by Senator Edward Kennedy. This report expressed the subcommittee members' shock at what they saw and heard as they traveled to all parts of the country and visited Indians in their homes and schools. At the conclusion of the report (U.S. Senate 1969:21), the committee characterized the dominant policy of the federal government toward Native Americans as one of "coercive assimilation," with historical roots in "a continuous desire to exploit, and expropriate, Indian land and physical resources" and "a self-righteous intolerance of tribal communities and cultural differences." This had resulted in a nation in which degrees of "prejudice, racial intolerance, and discrimination toward Indians [are] far more widespread and serious than generally recognized."

Furthermore, the report strongly censured federal Indian education policy. It described the education of Native Americans as "coercive assimilation" on the part of the dominant society. It explained that schools attended by Indian children had become a "kind of battleground where the Indian child attempts to protect his integrity and identity as an individual by defeating the purposes of the school." These schools had failed to "understand or adapt to, and in fact often denigrate, cultural differences." The schools were blaming "their own failures on the Indian student . . . which reinforces his defensiveness." The schools failed "to recognize the importance and validity of the Indian community." In addition, the community and the child retaliated "by treating the school as an alien institution." The report concluded by saying that the effect of this type of schooling had been a "dismal record of absenteeism, dropouts, negative self-image, low achievement, and, ultimately, academic failure for many Indian children."

The report included suggestions that Indian culture, history, and language be included as part of the school curriculum and that Indian parents become much more involved in the education of their children. These recommendations complemented demands that various American linguistic minority groups, including the Navajos and other tribes, were making for themselves and their children. The subcommitte's recommendations resulted in legislation authorizing bilingual education and English-as-a-second-language programs for "Limited English Proficient" students. Despite the claims made for the worth and importance of these bilingual programs in supporting native languages and cultures, the fact is that few of the programs addressed in good faith the concerns of reports such as the 1969 one. Most were *transitional* bilingual programs that were designed to facilitate students' transition from being monolingual or dominant speakers of their native language to being monolingual speakers of English. Only a very few had the goal of maintaining, much less improving, the students' native language proficiency.

For the Navajos, this decade brought confidence and a nationalistic mood. When, in 1969, the Advisory Committee of the Navajo Tribal Council passed a resolution officially calling for use of the term "Navajo Nation," Navajos were asserting a sovereignty derived from their existence as a recognized tribe and not from any grant or delegation of power from state or federal powers.

The 1960s and 1970s also saw Navajos and other Native Americans taking their first steps toward self-determination in education as their leaders began to apply their new awareness of sources of political power and financial support toward educational goals. They saw the need for establishing fundamental educational goals and identifying means for realizing them. Furthermore, as Gloria Emerson (1983:66) wrote, "many Navajos had graduated from colleges or were working on degrees. Some planned to wrest control from non-Indian school officials and staff, not only on the reservation but wherever there was a heavy enrollment of Navajo students."

These Navajo people were weary of government promises and excuses. For years, Anglo-dominated schools had failed to recognize unique Navajo needs and had disregarded the right of Indian parents and leaders to have a voice in policy formation and administration. This movement for self-determination, based on actual experience of the previous system, gave Navajo criticisms of the Western system the utmost legitimacy. The movement's goals were to revise this educational system into one that would be more responsive to Navajos' self-defined needs and that would be shaped and directed by their own people.

What was being proposed, in fact, was the revolutionary idea that it was time that the schools *for* Navajos, which had been functioning as sites for reproduction of the hegemony, should be transformed into schools *by* Navajos that would henceforth reproduce the Navajo counterhegemony. This new type of schooling, which had grown out of and in reaction to existing programs, was to take place in "contract schools," in which educational services would be contracted for by an established and recognized school board made up of local community members. Provisions for such an arrangement were outlined in Public Law 93-638, the Indian Self-Determination and Education Reform Act, enacted by the U.S. Congress in 1975.

Among the earliest and most successful contract schools was the famous Rough Rock Demonstration School, which was established in a small community where most people still followed the traditional Navajo pastoral lifestyle, shopped at the local trading post, spoke Navajo almost exclusively, and had little formal education and no previous contact with a school in their community. John Dick, one of the school's founders, explained the need for the bilingual and bicultural curriculum that was designed for it: "We want our children to be proud of being Navajos. We want them to know what they are. . . . In the future they will have to be able to make many children and do many things. They need a modern education to make their way, but they have to know both worlds—and being Navajo will give them strength" (Fuchs and Havighurst 1972:253).

A number of innovative policies were implemented at the Rough Rock school. Traditional people from the community were involved not only in policy decisions but also in teaching part of the Navajo cultural curriculum and living in the dormitories with the children. There was an open door policy that encouraged community members to observe and participate in the educational process. These people were also encouraged to use any of the school's resources. Anita Pfeiffer (1996) described how such schools also provided for nonacademic needs of the community. In addition to contributing agricultural and business expertise to communities, schools provided water, laundry facilities, and sewing machines. Such schools also became one of the biggest employers of Navajos on the reservation—first in menial jobs as janitors, cooks, and bus drivers, but later in professional positions as teachers, counselors, and administrators. In conjunction with schools such as Rough Rock, written Navajo language, history, and cultural curriculum materials were produced.

The role of Rough Rock Demonstration School as a model for other tribal education programs cannot be overemphasized. It was the school that established the legal precedent for the right of the federal government to give funds directly to local Indian communities to run their own schools. Inspired by its example, other Navajo contract schools were founded, including Ramah Navajo High School in New Mexico and Rock Point School in Arizona.

Navajo Community College (now known as Diné College), the first of the twenty-nine tribal colleges now operating in the United States, came into existence as a direct outgrowth of the successes at Rough Rock. For some time, the Navajo tribe had felt the need to establish its own institution of higher education so that Navajos who wanted a college education would not be forced to leave the reservation—and their homes and families—to attend college. According to Emerson (1983:669), many students found the curriculum at outside universities meaningless: "The type of technical assistance that the non-Indian colleges and universities were providing was fragmented and superficial." Also, many students could not afford to leave their homes and jobs, despite the availability of tribal scholarships. Therefore, in July 1968, Navajo Community College was created and chartered by the Navajo Tribal Council; it was the first Indian owned and operated college on an Indian reservation and the first to be fully accredited. It was also the first of the Navajo educational institutions to have the entire Navajo Nation as its fundamental community.

These Navajo-ized schools share a number of characteristics. Chief among them is the attempt to meet what are described as the unique needs of Navajo students and community members. These schools became very public sites in which Navajos were to challenge the dominance of Western values, culture, and models of doing business, via a process of "indigenization" (McLaughlin 1992:12). This indigenization of a state institution is the process that I suggest may be viewed as a powerful alteric strategy used by Navajos in constructing and asserting their distinctive ethnic identity, thus justifying a continuing "special" sovereign status—including the continued right to federal funding for Navajo-defined purposes.

One of the as-yet-unnamed consequences of the Western-type boarding and other schools that served the Navajos (and other Indian groups) between 1868 and the founding of the Navajo-controlled community schools was their success in disrupting the traditional or indigenous way of life without successfully assimilating Navajos into the mainstream United States.

Several characteristics of boarding schools should be stressed. One is that for many Navajo children, the boarding school experience started when they were quite young and continued into the students' late teens. Even during holidays and summers, when it might have been possible for students to return home to spend time with their families, they often were encouraged to stay at the school or nearby in order to take jobs and earn money. Often the period of formal schooling was followed by an interval of off-reservation job training or employment or both. This pattern assured that Navajo youths were separated from their families and home communities for large portions of their formative years.

This separation of students from their families and cultural origins was deliberate. Robert Trennert (1988:7) gives us Henry Pratt's own words in describing the Carlisle Indian School he had founded; it was "a self-contained unit that shut out all traditional Indian influences." Trennert (1988:7) continues, "The masthead of the school paper perhaps most succinctly stated Pratt's outlook: 'To Civilize The Indian; Get Him Into Civilization. To Keep Him Civilized; Let Him Stay.' To the innovative schoolmaster, returning a child to a tribal home was counterproductive, negating the basic purpose of his education and destroying individual initiative by placing him under the 'communistic government of the tribes.'"

With so many of the youth of the tribe absent, family members remaining at home no doubt contrived alternative ways of accomplishing the subsistence tasks and other necessities that formed part of the daily and seasonal round. The outcome of this forced, distant formal schooling was that the family and community pattern of life was irrevocably altered. Because young Navajos were available for traditional family and cultural socialization and teaching only during a relatively short period in their lives, others (the very young and the older members of the group) took over some of what would have been their roles and responsibilities. Even if these students were to return home to stay in the future, they would not easily be able to assume these or many of the other roles in the community.

While the traditional family structure was being assaulted, other changes were coming to the home communities back on the reservation. Trading posts were being built, even in the most remote locations. Markets were being created and then expanded for Navajo handicrafts as well as for livestock and raw wool. Navajo men were spending part of their year away from home working for wages on the encroaching railroads, and a cash economy was becoming commonplace. Catholic and Protestant missionaries were flocking to the reservation and staking their claims to exclusive territories. Hospitals and clinics were being built, and their services were being sought by many instead of, or in addition to, those of traditional medicine people, diagnosticians, and herbalists.

Due to these innovations, as well as those introduced by the schools, a number of the functions that had formerly been carried out within the extended family were beginning to be performed by these other institutions. Subsistence and other economic requirements of a family's life, along with medical and spiritual needs, were being met, for many, outside of the Navajo family and community. Then as now, there was little employment for Navajos—the *Navajo Times* recently reported a 45 percent unemployment rate (Donovan 1997:A-1)—and state and federal assistance contributed a great deal to meeting Navajos' physical and economic needs.

Another need—that of educating Navajo children—was also taken over by the federal government. Its policies regarding schools and curricula conformed to then-current theories about the roles Native Americans could be expected to play in American society. In order to suit Navajos for this projected life, the government, acting through BIA schools, provided for instruction in the basic academic subjects, in the Christian religion, in the English language, and, in most cases, in some sort of vocational program—usually something manual for boys and domestic for girls. Because the aim of the school programs was to totally transform the students' cultures, almost nothing was left to the parents, extended families, and communities.

Today, as Navajos work to redesign their schools so that Navajo-determined needs are met, rather than only those of the dominant society, questions are raised about the role of schools in maintaining and transmitting Navajo language and culture. These subjects are usually discussed together, though there are some areas of divergence.

Among the people I interviewed, there was near unanimity that, ideally, both Navajo language and culture should be taught by the family—if, in fact, the parents wished for their children to learn those things. A number of people, however, acknowledged that not all families had the knowledge, time, or ability to teach Navajo language and culture to children. Pauline Manygoats (pseudonym), an employee at Diné College, said she thought it was important for Navajo language and culture to be taught in school. She herself did not feel competent to teach her children all they needed to know:

Because some parents, we really don't know all of the stuff. Because our parents really never taught us all those stuff. They'll say it has to be holy, you know. It has to be this way. You have to be this way. Or either you can't say it now [this time of year]. You're not supposed to tell now or something like that. They just keep it to themself and especially way back, I guess they were been saying that to their kids, so it went on and on and on, so our parents really didn't got all the information and then when we're been raised, our parents didn't really know much about it, so they didn't teach us. So, teaching the Navajo culture at school is really good. (February 5, 1995)

Barbara Singer (pseudonym), also a member of the staff at Diné College, placed the blame on herself. She felt she and other working parents, particularly single mothers like her, were not doing all they should for their children. She described her own experience:

I think that us parents don't spend enough time with them, you know, like in the evenings with their homework or, you know, projects that they're doing at school. I think that's the main reason why [they aren't doing well in school]. Even sometimes I'm guilty of that, you know; I'm tired when I come home from work and I'm grouchy and, you know, I have to do all these other things, like cooking and cleaning up afterwards and trying to make sure that everything's OK for the next day and, you know, you're all tired out. And therefore, you know, I don't get to spend, you know, sit down and spend time with them, with their schoolwork. I think that's the main reason, you know, we don't have parent involvement with their children's education. . . . We're losing our language, I think, and our culture. I think that they should try to, I know like people my age, I know they know the teachings from our mothers, our dads, you know, grandparents, and so on, and I think they should pass those on to their younger kids. So that it doesn't, you know, lose our language and our culture. I think that's important, but, you know, again, like I said, we don't spend the time to teach them that. I know, they do need to spend more time with the kids and, I don't know, maybe they could bring grandma in or grandpa and have them tell stories to the children. (July 27, 1994)

These are among the reasons behind the belief held by many that Navajo lan-

guage and culture should be taught in Navajo schools. On the basis of her dissertation research among Navajo-speaking parents of the Hardrock Chapter in the Black
Mesa highlands of Arizona, Evangeline Parsons-Yazzie (1995:38) stated that the
parents she spoke with were unanimous: "The recommendations [they made] for
the maintenance and preservation of the Navajo language overwhelmingly placed
the task in the lap of the schools."

Alvina Tsosie agreed that schools could play an important role. She said,
"Navajo language should definitely be taught in school because of the danger
of the language dying out and also because young people need to know how to
speak it in order to have a full identity of themselves and their purposes of being
here. . . . No language leads to no more cultural ways which leads to nothing but
brown skin with no identities or clues as to who they are. I think that this can be
fixed if parents teach their kids and if the school curriculum allowed Navajo studies
to be implemented" (October 8, 1994).

Johnson Dennison concurred that this was necessary, saying, "In pertaining to
the cultures, I think a lot of the young people has the opportunity to develop the
sense of cultural respect, cultural knowledge. Because it is in the curriculum now"
(June 1, 1994).

There is, however, a fair amount of disagreement about exactly what consti-
tutes appropriate specific content within these broad areas. Content in the teaching of Navajo language is much less controversial than that of Navajo culture. Few
oppose the Navajo language's being offered in Navajo schools, but some parents
do not want Navajo language courses to be *required*. They feel that it should be
the parents' decision whether their children study the language or not. Paul Willeto
said, "To me there should be an all-out effort to put the responsibility back on the
families. You know, you, the families, you take the responsibility. Like me, I chose
to teach Navajo to Kim at a certain point. That's the choice *I* make. I shouldn't be
told, 'You're not teaching your kids Navajo.' Well, I'll listen to someone who tells
me that, but I'm going to say, 'Thank you, but I made a conscious decision to do
this.' Just like . . . certain families have decided to do certain things because of
this or that reason. They have the right. You know, there're certain movements
within the government and then so forth that have this feeling [that Navajo language instruction should be required in the schools]" (May 22, 1994).

Others approve of the teaching of the Navajo language so long as the instruction program has no religious or sacred content. This position tends to be characteristic of Navajo Christians.

The teaching of Navajo culture is much more problematic. Two quite different
factions oppose the teaching of the sacred and "religious" side of Navajo culture.

One of these factions is made up of Navajo Christians, who often support the teaching only of secular Navajo content. The other faction is that of Navajos who are whole-hearted believers in their traditional culture and who think its sacred content and language should not be taught lightly in a school setting. Partly because of the influence of these factions, in most Navajo culture programs on the Navajo Reservation, children are taught color names, numbers, and information about plants and animals, foods, arts and crafts, and everyday activities. In the winter, Coyote stories may be told. There is less likelihood that culture courses will include information about the Holy People, the four sacred mountains, the Emergence myth, or the Sa'ah Naagháí Bik'eh Hózhóón paradigm.

Della Toadlena expressed her view of this matter in the following words: "Stuff like weaving and moccasin making might be all right to teach, yeah. But anything that has to more with like the sacred stories and stuff I don't think should be taught in schools. Because that's sacred. It's sacred knowledge; it's guarded knowledge and it should remain in the home and each family then would practice it according to how they're been taught. I don't think it should be taught in the school" (September 27, 1994).

Greg Sarris (1993) described the existence of a similar ambivalence on the Kashaya Pomo Reservation when, following the suggestion of school board members who wanted students to learn "Indian values," a teacher introduced a traditional Kashaya story about Slug Woman into her reading class. The Anglo teacher wanted the students to feel proud of their background and thought that a story from their own culture might engage their interest, making them more attentive and successful in reading. She was horrified when some of the students reacted vehemently against the attempt:

> *"There's no such thing as Slug Woman," one student proclaimed. "That's all devil worship," another said. The scurrilous eight-year-old shouted, "I don't want to read about no savages." The few students who didn't protest were seemingly unimpressed. "It's just like a cartoon. Not real. Something like Peanuts," said one girl. Another student, a sixth grader, mentioned she had heard different versions of the story from her mother. She was going to ask her mother to talk more about Slug Woman. But, according to Bishop [the teacher], the girl never said another word about the subject in front of her classmates. Bishop went back to the standard reader. (Sarris 1993:173)*

Sarris discussed a complex array of explanations for the students' varied responses, and this chapter in his excellent book *Keeping Slug Woman Alive* (1993) is well worth reading. The point is that no generalizations can be made about the cultural and spiritual beliefs of any Native American group of individuals. The range is wide; the reasons are many. This variability makes it extremely difficult to develop school curricula that please and meet the needs of everyone.

Donald Denetdeal, the Navajo history instructor at Diné College and a Blessing Way singer, is somewhat unusual in his view that schools should play no role at all in teaching either Navajo language or culture. He explains: "I'm always against that and even in working with the BIA schools, I've spoken against it. I'm not a Navajo language advocate; I don't think it should be taught in school; it belongs at the home. It belongs with the Navajo family. If they want to preserve the language and if they want their children to speak Navajo, that should be left up to the home. That's the parents' responsibility, as well as culture, and school doesn't really have much to do with teaching the language and the culture" (February 15, 1996).

Despite these debates, there appears to be a consensus that Navajo language and culture are not being taught in Navajo homes. Furthermore, there appears to be great confidence among most Navajos that Navajo schools are equal to the task of teaching Navajo children so that the language and culture will be maintained and transmitted to future generations. This confidence seems to be based on a trust that schooling on the Navajo Reservation is sufficiently under the control and direction of the Navajos themselves to have become a truly Navajo institution with Navajo needs and desires underlying curricula and administrative policies.

A CLOSE LOOK AT A NAVAJO-IZED SCHOOL: DINÉ COLLEGE, TSAILE CAMPUS

One school that is consistently represented as being a very Navajo institution is Diné College. A description and analysis of the ways in which Diné College represents and demonstrates itself as thoroughly Navajo enables us to better evaluate the contributions that such an institution might make to the future of the Navajo language (and culture). The formal discourse circulated by Diné College forcefully communicates a counterhegemonic Navajo ideology. Each year's college catalog spells out the school's uniquely Navajo features:

> Educational Philosophy: Diné bi'óhóó'aah bítséílíé éí Sa'ąh Naagháí Bik'eh Hózhóón. Nitsáhákees, Nahat'á, liná dóó Sihasin t'áá shá bik'ehgo bee hahodét'é. Naayée'eek'ehgo na'nitin biné' oodáál dóó Hózhóójik'ehgo na'nitin bee hózhóógo oodáál. Díí bee óhoo'aah dóó naanish silá.

The educational philosophy of Diné College is Sa'ąh Naagháí Bik'e Hózhóón, *the Diné traditional living system, which places human life in harmony with the natural world and the universe. The philosophy provides principles both for protection from the imperfections in life and for the development of well-being.*

Mission statement: Diné College (formerly Navajo Community College) was established to meet the educational needs of the Navajo people. As the only academic postsecondary institution chartered by the Navajo Nation Council, the College offers two-year programs according to the needs of the Navajo Nation. The mission of the College is to:

- *Strengthen Personal Foundations for Responsible Learning and Living Consistent with* Sa'ąh Naagháí Bik'eh Hózhóón. *The college provides instruction and prepares students to have personal motivation and determination to clearly define and begin to develop their educational goals according to the protective and ethical values in* SNBH.
- *Prepare Students for Careers and Further Studies. The College prepares students for entry into the job market, provides courses that develop and upgrade college level skills, and offers academically challenging and transferable college level courses.*
- *Promote and Perpetuate Navajo Language and Culture. One unique function of Diné College is to promote, nurture, and enrich the language and culture of the Navajo people, in ways based on* Sa'ąh Naagháí Bik'eh Hózhóón.
- *Provide Community Services and Research. The College provides educational programs, research, leadership, and consulting services to address community needs. (Diné College 1997:1)*

The statement of the educational philosophy in both Navajo and English—especially giving Navajo precedence over English—the offering of instruction in Navajo philosophy and values, and the promotion of Navajo language and culture all mark the college as unique and special. In addition, the graduation requirements for its associate of arts degree include three credit hours of Navajo history, three of Navajo language, and three of Navajo culture. The college catalog offers fifteen Navajo language courses, ranging from "Navajo as a Second Language" to "Advanced Navajo Public Speaking" and "Navajo Descriptive Writing." There are nineteen Navajo and Indian Studies (NIS) courses, including those on Navajo pottery, basketry, weaving, silversmithing, and moccasin making. Other NIS courses are "Foundations of Navajo Culture," "Introduction to Navajo Herbology," "Navajo

Oral History," "Native American Wholistic *[sic]* Expression," and "Navajo Philosophy."

In addition, the Diné Educational Philosophy Office offers classes for faculty "to provide faculty with an introduction to SNBH teaching of the Diné knowledge and living systems; relate to curricula, pedagogy and academic life in higher educational learning. It is to allow faculty to learn the basic Diné Educational Philosophy as part of integration process meaningful for students to learn" (Diné College 1997:47). Having learned the basics of the Diné educational philosophy, including the SNBH paradigm, faculty members are required to implement this paradigm in their teaching of all their classes. This is something that all faculty—Navajo and non-Navajo—must agree to do in their employment contracts; moreover, the annual renewal of faculty contracts is supposedly contingent upon the instructor's having carried out this requirement.

Furthermore, the college offers associate of arts degrees in Navajo culture, Navajo language, and Navajo bilingual-bicultural education. A recent development is a partnership between the college's Diné Teacher Education Program and Arizona State University in offering a bachelor of arts degree in elementary education. Unique features of this program are an entrance requirement of oral fluency in Navajo language and coursework taught in Navajo, as well as requirements for junior- and senior-year students to write papers in Navajo.

Diné College identifies itself as a Navajo institution in many other ways as well. First, as the college catalog explains, "The Tsaile, *'Tsééhili,'* Campus, designed in the circular, holistic tradition of the Navajo hogan, reflects the strength and dignity of the rich Navajo culture. Administrative, instructional, housing, recreational, cafeteria and library facilities are accurately placed in reference to traditional Navajo beliefs; thus, creating an environment for traditional growth and academic success" (Diné College 1997:2). A number of individual buildings on the campus also take the octagonal shape of the traditional Navajo dwelling, the hogan; these include the cafeteria, the two-story library building, and the Ned Hatathli Center (also known as the Culture Center), a six-story bronze glass–sheathed structure housing the administrative offices, the college museum, an interior hogan with a small wood stove and a dirt floor, and some classrooms. The college also maintains a small, traditional log hogan south of the imposing glass Culture Center; it "serves as a place of sacred ceremonials performed for the college's staff, faculty, students, and the college itself" (Aronilth n.d.:36).

The walls and hallways of all of the buildings are decorated with large murals depicting scenes from traditional Navajo life, familiar landscapes, events from the Emergence myth or more recent Navajo history (the Long Walk, for instance), and representations of Talking God and other Holy People. In addition, individual offices are ornamented with paintings, calendars, and posters with Navajo themes; artifacts such as cradleboards, pottery, and coiled wedding baskets; Navajo rugs or other weavings; and carvings and sand-painting pictures.

Navajo faculty and staff, male and female, wear Navajo jewelry; those with long hair occasionally wear it in the traditional *tsiiyééł*. On ceremonial or other special occasions (such as Indian Day), people wear moccasins and women sometimes wear flounced skirts and velveteen blouses, sash belts, and concho belts.

Formal public events are routinely marked as Navajo by the use of greetings, clan introductions, and opening and closing prayers. If the Navajo language is used at all in such events, these are the speech genres that prompt the use of the language. On occasion, people making speeches will use Navajo for a portion of their speech. With any of these uses of Navajo, except for prayers, it is common for the speaker then to repeat the contents of the greeting or introduction in English. There is a tendency for the extended Navajo performances, such as prayers, to be carried out by the same Navajo language or culture instructors at event after event. The foregoing uses of the language are noncontroversial. The use of Navajo is, however, highly unusual and controversial when it is used to conduct college business when nonspeakers of the language are present. Many Navajos, especially women, label this behavior "rude" and inappropriate for "professional" matters because it excludes nonspeakers.

The use of the Navajo language is otherwise not particularly marked. It is much more common among the staff members—janitors, maintenance and cafeteria workers, and secretaries. Navajo-speaking faculty and administrators rarely use the language at school unless they wish to signal solidarity or to mark an event as Navajo; English is by far the norm.

Except in the Diné Teacher Education Program and the Navajo and Indian studies classes, Navajo is rarely used as a primary language of instruction in Diné College classes. When it is used in NIS classes such as Foundations of Navajo Culture or Navajo Philosophy, speech in Navajo is immediately followed by translation of the content. Non-Navajo-speaking students routinely take these courses and are able to perform quite well without any proficiency at all in Navajo.

In addition to the various ways in which the physical plant and activities of Diné College are marked as distinctly and "authentically" Navajo, a great deal of counterhegemonic discourse is performed on every possible public college occasion. To illustrate the sort of alteric identity-building discourse performed at Diné College, I have selected two representative contexts. The first is the large public event in which college officials describe the unique features of this, the first and largest of America's tribal colleges. The former president of the college, Tommy Lewis, was unflagging in his efforts to depict Diné College as alteric; his twin themes were the unique status conveyed upon the college by its traditional Navajo educational philosophy and the belief that, because of that philosophy, Diné College was equal, if not superior, to any other institution of higher learning. At the Tsaile commencement ceremony on May 6, 1994, Lewis explained that "it is a hard task to administer this institution of ours. It is special and unique; there is no other one like it in the world. It is special because of the philosophy, our own traditional teaching based on our language and culture. Our curriculum and instruction and the way that we carry out our lives are based on SNBH. Our education is one of a kind. . . . Navajo Community College is one of the best colleges found anywhere because of the SNBH."

The next year, at a general student assembly on September 9, 1995, he said, "NCC is one of the finest institutions in the world; its educational philosophy is unique and different. . . . The sky's the limit; you can do it. The teaching here prepares you for foundation. CDS [Center for Diné Studies], Navajo teaching is a strong part of our curriculum. Education on the reservation has been off tangent in the last twenty years. We want to get back on track with education the way it should have been."

And finally, at the new student orientation on September 9, 1996, he offered this assessment of the college: "We're at par with what's expected at other educational institutions. Our students come out shining. The proof is one-to-one transfer, to be at par. We're with Harvard, Yale, and other prestigious universities. Tribal colleges rank at high level throughout the country. NCC is a big player in tribal issues as the biggest and oldest tribal college."

The other discourse context I want to represent here is that of the classes offered by the Diné Educational Philosophy Office. There, two Navajo culture experts, Anthony Lee, Sr., and Frank Morgan, use discourse in a problem-solving sense. They use discourse that is alteric in content to define and then address the chief problem they (and others) see as afflicting the Navajo people—the negative impact of Western society on the Navajo people. First, they establish that in the old (precontact) days, Navajos had the solutions to all their problems in their oral history, ceremonies, prayers, relationship with nature, k'é and clan system, and community closeness and interrelationships. They knew how to keep everything in balance using the teachings given to them by the Holy People.

With Western contact, many new goods and practices were brought to the land between the sacred mountains. Some things were imposed on the Navajos, but others they consciously chose. The Navajo people thought there would be a balance between the new things and the old, but the situation got out of hand—out of balance, distorted, and disrupted. This was because the Anglos took charge and forced things on the Navajos. Also, some Navajos became attracted to and dependent on practices and items that were bad for them, such as alcohol, gambling, welfare, and the leveling of the sexual division of labor and spheres of activity. These were abused by the Navajos who used them to excess. Therefore, many of the Navajo people's real problems today come from Western innovations and their subsequent misuse.

Frank Morgan explained how this all happened:

According to Hózhóójik'ehgo hane' [Blessing Way teachings], from outside of the four sacred mountains, there are other Indians and Westerners. This is fine; they are in our prayers. . . . [There are things out there that we would like.] We ask for them. We say, "Shoosąą dooleeł, they have an affinity for me; I attract them." We pray for them. You think, assume that these are good. If you don't handle them right, they become harmful. You create an imbalance. There are some things we shouldn't bring in—TV, videos, tribal government, gambling, drugs. Those things are harmful, whatever you do with them. (February 7, 1995)

We need to improve and have these things [that have come in from outside] blessed by others. Bring in improvements. It's the same thing with education—bring it in and make it consistent with teachings. Government brought it in and eradicated Navajo. Navajos thought it would be an equal basis. Old chiefs were speaking like that. . . . Our education comes from that treaty and we didn't take it so it would eliminate our ways. We took it so it would improve our ways. That's the way it should have been. . . . In the 1880s, government education came in and until 1950 it was the policy to take culture away and to eliminate Navajo language. They replace it with curriculum from the outside. . . . [Raymond] Nakai [a former Navajo Nation chairman] and others wanted real education. Take Western education a whole different direction and base it on Navajo education. This is what they wanted, to improve nitsáhákees [thinking], nahat'á [planning], iiná [life, implementation], sihasin [evaluation, confidence or competence]. Notice other problems— there are single parents, they didn't know their clans, people got together out at those schools, like Intermountain. Leaders began to feel the effects of it. There was lots of alcoholism. There were people who did not have any discipline. They were unapproachable; couldn't straighten them out. They needed an education based on Navajo education. (February 28, 1995)

The solution to these and other Navajo problems is for the old ways to be brought back and for people to live by them. This sort of cultural revitalization would correct the problems, Morgan and Lee said. Lee elaborated on this theme: "There are four sacred mountains. There's something significant about that place.

Those people didn't live like the Diné today. They survived and were self-sufficient. Everything was natural then. No commodities or social assistance. The people didn't live as we do today. We can't totally relive those ways, but we can reestablish the essence of what they lived and survived with" (February 28, 1995).

It is clear that many Navajo families are not teaching their children how to live their lives in this sense; they are not teaching the "old ways." Family members work outside the home; parents and others do not model what young people should be learning. Some parents and grandparents do not know the old ways or the language themselves and therefore cannot pass it on to the youth.

Frank Morgan contrasted life with and without the traditional teachings: "Older people have a lot of expansive, extensive, comprehensive thinking. They were raised that way; now children grow up in a working environment—Bashas', tribe, etc. Children are latchkey—out of that environment; they don't go through that discipline. They don't learn how to do things. . . . If students are more traditional, it could work that way. [They could find the answers to their problems in the traditional stories]. Over half of them don't know their teaching" (January 31, 1995; April 4, 1995).

Therefore, according to this line of thinking, schools need to take over the teaching function to teach students how to bring back the "old ways" and apply them in their lives. Morgan described the period in the 1960s when "things began to change to be the way it is now. . . . With all these things, let's create a college and see if we can maintain it. Bring in Western knowledge and discipline and learn good things from it. We are aware of mainstreaming, but we don't want to replace the old ways with Western ways. Our mission—all of us—is to contribute to the revitalization of this" (January 31, 1995).

Furthermore, it is said, in order for schools to accomplish the goal of teaching students the old ways, the schools themselves need to be more Navajo, the way they should have been in the first place. Only a Navajo school can fit the Navajo mind of Navajo students. That unique mind is there; it just needs to be reactivated by Navajo teachings. In addition, Navajo teachers, a Navajo perspective ("Do it from a Navajo perspective—that's who you're dealing with"), and Navajo history, culture, and language are needed to reach Navajo students. This, these educators say, is what it would take for a truly Navajo school, which Diné College is believed to be, to counteract Western damage.

Diné College, "the higher education institution of the Navajo Nation," has, over the years, undergone a counterhegemonic, ideology-driven transformation. The surface aspects of the college—its architecture, its decorations, its course offerings, its discourse—represent this institution as the site of present and future Navajo language (and culture) maintenance and preservation. However, a closer examination of this institution (among many others) reveals a disparity between its ostentatious Navajo-ness (visible in public performances and physical manifestations) and its actual achievements in producing Navajo language fluency (among students who were not already speaking the language) and intergenerational transmission of language (and culture) within the family. This situation is characteristic of many Navajo language and culture teaching and support efforts of the Navajo Nation. Recognizing this disparity (and the ideological diversity and contestation it represents) is an important step toward designing and implementing more effective Navajo language and culture programs.

A NAVAJO PARADIGM FOR REVERSING NAVAJO LANGUAGE SHIFT

SIX

One of the weaknesses inherent in many of the past and present language programs on the Navajo Reservation that teach either Navajo or English or both, and also with programs that purport to work toward the maintenance of the Navajo language, is that they are predicated on an ideology that holds one language (either Navajo or English) and one culture to be obviously superior to the other in almost every possible way. The "other" language and its metonymically associated culture are, therefore, necessarily inferior. This is the opposition in action. In most language programs on the reservation, it appears that schools have been far more successful in achieving the unstated ideological goal—that of valorizing and legitimating Navajo culture and its associated language at the expense of all other cultures and languages—than in reaching the ostensible goal of maintaining or even advancing Navajo culture and language knowledge and practice. The emphasis has been on image over substance; for the Navajo Nation as a whole, actual progress in halting or reversing language shift has been minimal. Each succeeding Navajo Nation language survey tells the tale.

In the past (except during the Collier era of the 1930s), most language programs on the Navajo Reservation, including bilingual programs, were geared toward teaching English language and Western culture—values and assumptions—as quickly and efficiently as possible. The goal of such programs was the eventual irreversible assimilation of Navajo students into mainstream American culture—albeit at an economically and socially disadvantaged level. This goal was to be accomplished by replacing the students' native language and home culture with those of the dominant society; an underlying goal was to inculcate a belief in the innate inferiority of their own language and culture and a desire to shake them off in order to progress to the infinite advantages of modernity and "civilization." Students who had successfully been reprogrammed to embrace the American way were then to be instruments of conversion in their families and communities, if and when they returned "home." The superiority of English and the American lifestyle was thought to be self-evident. This is a classic hegemonic position and a classic means of hegemonic incorporation.

When federally funded bilingual programs were introduced on the reservation, Navajos hailed them as evidence that the worth and viability of the Navajo language had at last been recognized. Many of the founders and personnel of these early programs praised this bilingual innovation as the key to Navajo students' successful adaptation to their transformed homeland; it would allow students to take the best from both worlds. As Hoke Denetsosie (1977:101) said, "For we members of our older generation we have done our part! Today, opportunities for improvement in life constitute a challenge for Navajo youth. Every Navajo child should have the benefit of learning our Navajo ways as well as those of the dominant society. Only by being exposed to both Navajo and Anglo cultures can we be able to distinguish and understand the good things, and the aspects that are not good, about each. One of our traditional Navajo leaders once said, 'Navajo schools should strive to prepare their students for life in the modern world, while, at the same time, keeping the best of Navajo tradition and culture.' I think that is wise and fitting."

Like Yup'ik people facing similar programs in Alaska (Henze and Vanett 1993:128), many Navajos believed that a chief goal of these bilingual programs was the maintenance of their language. However, the objective of the transitional bilingual model (by far the prevalent model) as defined by federal and state departments of education was to move children out of their native language and into English as quickly as possible. Despite extensive evidence demonstrating that only a minimal communicative competence could be achieved during this period of time, the usual duration of a school's bilingual component was four years (Crawford 1994).

The apparent (though unstated) goal of a number of the more recent language and culture programs on the Navajo Reservation has been the opposite of the English language–American culture mandate: they seek to demonstrate the cultural and moral bankruptcy of Western society and to inculcate a belief in the overall superiority of the Navajo language and culture. Neither of these agendas has been successfully accomplished, and I am not convinced that either has the best interests of its students at heart. Both emphasize chiefly one language, and both have been extreme, requiring either/or decisions of students. In earlier days, the choice was represented as between being an "American" (a modern person, a civilized person, a progressive person with a secure future, all of which are good) or being a "savage" (going "back to the blanket" and so on, which is a bad thing). In the 1990s, I heard Navajo students at Diné College describe the images of Navajo-ness available to them still in terms of opposites. On one hand, they can choose to "know who they are and where they come from" and be a "real Navajo," identifying themselves as such through their speech, dress, and activities. On the other, they can dress the way other American youths do, openly concentrate on their studies and career goals, and risk being labeled an "apple Indian" (red on the outside, white on the inside), a sell-out, and a traitor. Finding a balance between those two extreme cultural images of Navajo-ness continues to be a difficult task; alternatives to these extreme images are not widely recognized or discussed.

This is unfortunate, as Donna Deyhle's (1995) extensive research in schools in Navajo Reservation border communities illustrates. Chief among her many valuable insights and conclusions is this: "The more academically successful Navajo students are more likely to be those who are firmly rooted in their Navajo community" (Deyhle 1995:419). This finding stands in direct opposition to the philosophy behind most past as well as most contemporary schools for Navajos. Deyhle states this view succinctly: "The Anglo community views assimilation as a necessary path to school success. In this view, the less 'Indian' one is, the more academically 'successful' one will become."

In dichotomizing the choices, school programs (and other agents of change) are asking students to make impossible decisions. And students are well aware, on some deep level, of the disadvantages and oversimplifications in such choices. Despite the attractiveness of traditional Navajo beliefs and teachings, they see that choosing a "pure" Navajo option is unfeasible in the present world—sheepherding and growing a small garden, living in a hogan, and driving a team of horses are neither economically viable nor satisfying to most youths of today. Yet this is the lifestyle that is touted as perfection in most Navajo language and culture courses. On the other hand, however much they want economic security, interesting and challenging jobs, and material possessions, students can listen to the radio (KTNN, the tribal radio station broadcasting out of Window Rock, among others), watch television, and read newspapers (including their own *Navajo Times*) and recognize that contemporary American society has plenty of serious disadvantages—crime, disrespect for people, lack of direction and purposefulness.

When choices are presented as such polar opposites, students (and all of us, for that matter) are bound to experience conflict and indecision, both resistance and attraction. When no feasible choice seems possible, one is tempted to make no choice at all, to merely drift through life, to give up in the face of obstacles, to be guided by others, perhaps into a violent and self-destructive lifestyle. This lack of positive direction is precisely how some elders characterize many Navajo young people today.

Another possibility for Navajo youth is to accept the either/or dichotomy that they are presented with and to choose whichever appears to be the most desirable (though flawed) option. For most Navajos who have accepted the inevitability of the narrow range of options described to them by their school counselors and advisors, these "choices" have moved them in the direction of assimilation into the dominant society—which often, though not always, includes marrying outside the tribe, speaking only English and teaching only English to their children, living and working off the reservation, converting to Christianity or another nontraditional religion, and so on. When such assimilation has been "successful," these individuals become indistinguishable, except for their physical appearance, from the American mainstream. As Deyhle (1995:436) pointed out, however, the persistence of a racially defined job ceiling and "an Anglo-controlled social landscape that restricts employment opportunities for Navajo" is unlikely to allow particularly satisfactory employment experiences on or off the reservation.

The opposite, most purely alteric, choice would be a wholly traditional Navajo lifestyle. Although I have heard a number of Diné College students speak quite favorably about the *idea* of living the traditional lifestyle of their ancestors, I have no evidence that this positive attitude has actually translated to the *practice* of a purely traditional lifestyle by any of these students. Indeed, the students in a class in the Diné Teacher Education Program denied that any Navajos still lived a purely traditional lifestyle, free from Western borrowing.

Deyhle (1995:438) felt more confident than I do that "traditional Navajo cultural values still frame, shape, and guide appropriate behavior in the Navajo community." She described a much more favorable and culturally intact picture of the Navajo way of life in her study area than I am accustomed to hearing or seeing when she wrote that "life in homes on the reservation, surrounded by family, friends, and similar 'others,' is a sound choice for youth, with or without school credentials. The choice to remain on the reservation represents failed attempts to find security and happiness in towns and cities amid racial isolation and under- or unemployment. This choice also represents an ethical commitment and valuing of families and Navajo traditions. The Navajo community provides a place of social acceptance and economic survival unavailable in Anglo-dominant communities off the reservation."

There are certainly areas where Navajo culture and tradition, to greater and lesser degrees, prevail. Representations of contemporary Navajo life in Navajo media and in conversations and student writing, however, also depict a nation in which substance abuse, family violence and other evidence of dysfunctional behaviors, incest and abuse, jealousy, and gangs and other youth disturbances, as well as all manner of other hardships, exist. This is a setting in which not even the many strengths of Navajo tradition are solving all the problems.

I believe, then, that current tribal and educational discourse, which advances a Navajo/Western opposition, offers extreme choices, neither of them completely viable, neither of them realistic. Language and culture programs that deal in such essentialist and inadequate currency can only contribute to continued social dis-ease and disorder, and therefore to greater and faster Navajo language shift.

In crafting nativized schools and appropriate curricula for such schools, inno-vators must be aware of a number of social and political factors. In their discussion of the role of Yup'ik schools in language and culture maintenance, Rosemary Henze and Lauren Vanett (1993:130) described characteristic pitfalls that are equally appli-cable to Navajo schools:

> The school, then, is seriously compromised when it takes on, implicitly or explicitly, the role of mediator between traditional Yup'ik and Western culture. The school is biased by its very history as a Western institution. In our stu-dents, we found many instances of ambivalence in the school's attempts to promote Yup'ik language and culture. To expect the school and the layers of authority that govern the school to perform a mediating role is to invite bias and dilute the effects of cultural or language maintenance projects. The communities that really want to revitalize their language and culture would do better to turn to their own members: the parents of the children now in school. The school can and should do its part to be supportive, but the limitations of that part must be recognized.

It would be wise, when examining the Navajo educational situation, also to question the suitability of purely Western models of analysis, diagnosis, and pre-scription for Navajo language shift. Few are questioning the fact that the bulk of research, analysis, and prescribing is being done by non-Navajos (albeit some are individuals who have married into the tribe). Few are asking what Navajos (in the trenches, as it were) believe about even the possibility of Navajo language shift, much less what to do about it. Although I am indeed one more Anglo examining this issue and suggesting an approach, my attempt is to bring together Navajo points of view (in Navajos' own words) for Navajos to read and consider. Further, I am pro-posing that Navajos themselves consider the advantages of using their own Sa'ąh Naagháí Bik'eh Hózhóón paradigm in addressing this shift.

Whatever non-Navajo linguists or anthropologists or educators believe about the beauty, the interest, the valuable diversity, and the global importance of the languages of others (Krauss 1996), we must acknowledge that Western perspec-tives are not the only ones possible and that unless we choose to continue to impose our own values and choices on others (which we certainly have a long and highly effective history of doing), the ultimate fate of the Navajo language is not, and should not be, in our hands. Many Navajos do consider language a form of communal property—but it is Navajo property, not universal property. Navajos are making and will continue to make decisions about this linguistic property for themselves. In the eyes of many Navajos, the only appropriate roles for non-Navajos are to provide them with information to do with as they will and to assist them, if and when the outsiders are asked to do so. To insist that we outsiders know better than they is to persist in our classic paternalistic and imperialistic mode.

THE SA'ĄH NAAGHÁÍ BIK'EH HÓZHÓÓN PARADIGM

I want to suggest an alternative to the usual Western prescriptions for reversing Navajo language shift, one that is in keeping with the core of traditional Navajo philosophy and belief. This alternative is a teaching consistent with an ideology that elevates neither traditional Navajo nor American mainstream language and culture at the expense of the other. This model, instead, extols the virtue and the value of balance and harmony. It could, in short, create and maintain a true and equal bilingualism and mutually respectful biculturalism.

Such a model is intrinsically Navajo. Unlike any other one I have seen proposed, it is capable of addressing the diversity, contestation, and denial that have been omitted from other models. This model, in all aspects of Navajo life, gives people a way of acknowledging the conflict, the difficulties, the chaos, and the contradictions in their lives. It acknowledges that these unsettling forces are normal; they have always been present in Navajo life, and they have been dealt with again and again in the past. As Donald Denetdeal teaches in his Navajo history class at Diné College, Navajo history (despite the efforts of modern-day apologists) has never been free of conflict, hardship, and strife. Navajos have always been moving, changing, adapting, coping with the more rigorous and brutal forms of upheaval and displacement. That they have persisted, even thrived, into the present century is ample testimony to their cultural strength and centeredness.

The paradigm I am referring to is known as Sa'ąh Naaghái Bik'eh Hózhóón. In this chapter, I refer to it as the SNBH paradigm. I abbreviate the name for two reasons: a Western reason is that the whole name is long and cumbersome (especially to a non-speaker of Navajo); a Navajo reason is that the words of the Navajo phrase are extremely sacred and powerful and should not be spoken—or, one presumes, written—casually or frequently. This SNBH paradigm has provided in the past and is fully capable of continuing to provide a process for coping with the vicissitudes of life. Unfortunately, one of the harsh realities of contemporary Navajo life is that many Navajo young people no longer know their culture and its teachings and do not have knowledge of this paradigm as a resource to bring to bear on their troubles and challenges.

In recommending that Navajos employ the SNBH paradigm in addressing the problem of reversing language shift, I am also suggesting that the very use of it will illustrate or exemplify the strength and value the paradigm can bring to approaching life, and such use may influence others who observe the paradigm in action. To whatever extent the paradigm is successful in providing a foundation for reversing language shift, it will likewise be successful in assisting the reversal of culture shift by teaching the content and demonstrating the application of traditional Navajo values and practices in contemporary life. It has the potential for creating a snowball effect for the Navajo language in a direction opposite to its present decline.

As I propose this model, I am of course aware that SNBH originates in Navajo philosophical and spiritual traditions. These traditions have provided and, for many, continue to provide a pattern for living and structuring relationships among all aspects of creation. The traditional narratives and ceremonies that embody the teachings of this lifestyle deal with Holy People and other beings. Some contemporary factions consider these teachings, with their associated beliefs and practices, to be "religious," and they embrace or reject them on that basis. Other factions consider the nonceremonial aspects of this system merely a "life way" and see no conflict between it and other "religious" traditions.

The way it was explained to me by my various teachers is that only selected harmless aspects of the whole body of knowledge and practice that make up SNBH are used in educational settings. As I explain in greater detail later, the portions that have been excerpted for use with malleable young minds and spirits are those associated with the basic aspects of the natural world we live in. In this basic form, they offer a process for living a positive life and a system for relating to others.

It is true some will continue to oppose the use of this paradigm on grounds that it is incompatible with the Christian or other religious beliefs of some Navajos, as well as on the opposite grounds that its sacredness in the Navajo way makes it inappropriate in a school setting. Probably no paradigm exists that would not be objectionable to one group or another among the Navajo Nation, as is equally true anywhere else. Yet appears to me, as well as to many Navajos, that the potential advantages of implementing this paradigm outweigh its disadvantages and that it certainly has much to recommend it over the assimilationist and other models inflicted on the Navajos by Western educators and politicians.

DYNAMIC PROCESS: BALANCE AND HARMONY IN DUALITY

The SNBH teachings that follow are an integrated summary of material from a number of different sources within Diné College and the Tsaile community. At the time I conducted most of my research, Frank

Morgan, Anthony Lee, Sr., and Johnson Dennison made up the Diné Educational Philosophy (DEP) Office at Navajo Community College. In that capacity, they taught a class—DEP 294—to faculty in order to assist them in using the paradigm to organize and implement their course content—a mandate by the college Board of Regents. In addition to offering this course, the three men were joined by poet Rex Lee Jim in providing a number of workshops and seminars to educational, health services, and other professionals throughout the Navajo Reservation and surrounding communities. I also have extensive interview data from each of these men, as well as information from a number of more or less informal conversations. Johnson Dennison, a practicing medicine man for seventeen years, was particularly kind and helpful in explaining things to me and in correcting my spelling.

Another source for this information was Harry Walters, director of the Ned Hatathli Museum and the Center for Diné Studies and also a practicing medicine man. Walters was the instructor for the Navajo oral history class I took and one of the people I interviewed. Furthermore, he was consistently generous and patient with my requests for clarification of difficult concepts.

The Diné College instructor with whom I studied the most was Wilson Aronilth, a traditional medicine man as well as a Native American Church roadman. I have known him for more than fifteen years and have learned a great deal from him. Because he teaches his classes in both Navajo and English and tailors them specifically to a Navajo audience, I was given the unique opportunity to experience the challenges and, occasionally, the frustrations of being the linguistic and cultural minority—the only non-Navajo—in a classroom setting. In the first year or two, Aronilth occasionally used my difficulties with Navajo phonology to illustrate to the class the common observation that Anglos cannot pronounce Navajo.

These gentlemen, then, provided the information and the interpretative perspective on the Navajo material that follows. This material is written here very closely to the way it was presented to me. In the contexts in which I heard it, the intent of sharing this material was clearly pedagogical. In the absence of Navajo elders telling traditional "winter stories" and lecturing the youth far into the night, Diné College's Navajo and Indian studies classes, workshops, and seminars attempt to address that need. After all, Harry Walters told me, the purpose of these teachings is not to analyze them; it is to learn how to live in balance and harmony.

As translated by Frank Morgan (Febuary 7, 1995), *sa'* means "old age"; *ąh* means "up to; a long ways to and beyond." *Naa* means "around; cyclical; repetitive"; *ghái,* "it walks there." *Bi* means "its" (third person singular, possessive); *k'eh,* "according to; in line with; in sync with." *Hó* means "there is; the whole place"; *zhóón* means "beauty; balance; harmony; the way; the path of balance or harmony or beauty." Morgan's free translation of Sa'ąh Naagháí Bik'eh Hózhóón is "past old age, the one that walks there in ultimate balance and harmony or on the balanced path." This is sometimes shortened and referred to as "long-life happiness."

Therefore, SNBH refers to a life that is characterized by the balanced and harmonious interrelationship of male (Sa'ąh Naagháí) Protection Way and female (Bik'eh Hózhóón) Blessing Way aspects, which comprise everything that exists in the four directions of the natural world. You are told that you were created in the center of this natural world; you are in the center of earth and above. The center goes everywhere you go; it never changes. Furthermore, all things in this natural world—elements, people, animals, plants, heavenly bodies, daily phenomena—are SN. They all live in a balanced, interconnected, and ordered way within a BH system. All these entities around you—mountains, clouds, rains, sun, moon, lightning, stars, Holy People, sacred places within mountains and in canyons, the sun and moon, dawn, yellow twilight, blue twilight—have male and female relationships everywhere you see. These primal principles are inherent in the physical, cognitive, behavioral, perceptual, and spiritual makeup of all entities (including humans) and in their interrelations with one another.

It is said that it is important that you understand this natural order so that you can use it as a guide to the decisions and choices you will face in your life. When you are born, you are at the beginning of the Corn Pollen Path of Life. You want to get to 102 years—which is the culmination of a long, happy, and fruitful life—in good condition and remain in balance with everything. There are certain things that you want to have and achieve in that life. Family, home, livelihood, kinship, community, the Navajo Nation, the world outside—wherever you go, you are to live by this teaching and find good things out there and bring them home. That is what the elders say. Then, when you reach 102, you will be accepted by nature again; you are going back to nature. You will become everything that is good again. You are a child of nature and nature will take you back and reestablish you; you will become good things again. However, if you have not taken care of yourself, it is not good; it is negative.

Male principles in nature can be characterized as those that are powerful in strength, short-term in effect, destructive, protective, hard, negative, disciplinary, and capable of detecting harm. They are found in the Protection Way (Naayée'eek'ehgo na'nitin) teaching principle associated with the Sa'ąh Naagháí (SN) aspect of SNBH. This teaching originates in the natural world and guides us in recognizing danger and obstacles in our paths, and therefore it allows us to protect ourselves against them. It inculcates awareness of the self and surroundings in order to detect sources of difficulties and to identify and analyze problems in a productive way. Protection Way teachings instill security and inner strength and provide firm foundations in life. They shield us and deflect the harmful things that disrupt harmony and get us off the ethical balanced path. Once we identify harmful or disruptive things, we can take care of them and they will leave us alone. We can carry or wear protection elements in the form of jewelry with male turquoise and female white shell. These precious stones cast a mistlike aura around us. They are *bine'adzíjh,* meaning "behind this, one is safe and secure." We are hidden there, imperceptible to others because of these things. Other sources of protection are corn pollen and the little crystals taken from where lightning hits trees (Frank Morgan, February 14, 1995).

Nothing, however, is in perfect balance. There are always things that are a little off balance, which is why you need *naayée'* teaching for protection. Frank Morgan translates naayée' as "disharmony, problems, conflict, anything that's going to be harmful to you." This is also the word meaning monsters, such as the monsters in traditional Diné origin history (Yé'iitsoh, "the Giant," Tsédahódzíiłałii, "Monster That Kicked People Off the Cliff," Tsé Nináhalééh, "Monster Bird," and Hunger, Poverty, Sleep, Lice Man, Old Age, and others). Such naayée' knowledge can be used for good as described above, or it can be used to harm and for evil purposes. There are both good and evil in nature. There can also be good things that you do not use correctly—food, exercise, or thinking; they can be used to create a conflict and come back to harm you. When people say there is a cosmic natural order, this is what they mean.

The other side, or complement, of Protection Way is the Blessing Way, or Hózhóójík'ehgo na'nitin. These female principles are associated with the Bik'eh Hózhóón aspect of SNBH. They emphasize the way in which the natural world is "really beautifully put together" (Frank Morgan, March 7, 1995), as well as the means to restore elements in life to harmony and balance according to the cosmic natural order set down by the Holy People. Blessing Way principles are described as those that are weak to moderate in strength, long-term in effect, corrective, nourishing, soft, positive, ethical, compassionate, and capable of resolving issues or situations. These teachings allow you to recognize and attract good and positive things in life or valuable possessions that will enrich your life and bring you well-being and happiness.

Protection Way and Blessing Way are paired as male and female for a reason. We humans do not have the authority to mix things up. We are ourselves Holy People according to Navajo stories; therefore, we are supposed to be guided by examples of what they did before to maintain the natural order that they set in place for us.

These teachings work in conjunction with one another. After someone identifies and analyzes a problem using the Protection Way, for example, Blessing Way teachings are directed at setting up solutions to the problem. Together they result in balance, cohesion, and a bond. They are in balance; they do not exist apart; they are highly interconnected. These principles of duality come together in Navajos' central internal governing structures, which regulate their conduct, attitudes, personalities, behaviors, and perceptions. In addition, they have been put in place to further regulate Navajos' relationships with other individuals in a pattern that radiates out from the nuclear family core through the extended family, into the community of kinship and clanship, through the Navajo Nation, and beyond.

In conjunction with the patterns and teachings of duality that are associated with male and female components of SNBH, there is another set of related patterns and teachings that are associated with the four cardinal directions—east, south, west, and north, in that order. These principles act in the world as a four-phase process that is dynamic, cyclical, and connected to all aspects of nature. The movement of these principles is always sunwise (or clockwise). You do not mix them up; they have to be kept in their natural order. Each of these four phases has four aspects, each also associated with the cardinal directions. Within each of the four aspects, there are four more aspects, again associated with the four directions (Frank Morgan, February 28, 1995; March 7, 1995).

This is not the place to set out every detail of the four directions and all that is associated with them. I describe and discuss this natural process only to the extent necessary to provide the background for understanding the model I am suggesting.

The initial processual phase in the SNBH paradigm is found in the east and is associated variously with birth, white early morning dawn, the sacred White Shell Mountain, Sisnaajiní (Blanca Peak in Colorado, close to the New Mexico border), spring, and *nitsáhákees,* interpreted as "thinking, bringing to mind, recalling or recollecting, making conclusions and decisions, and having the mind go steadily toward action" (Frank Morgan, March 7, 1995).

It is by means of the elements of air and water, which regulate the processes of nitsáhákees, that a person is connected to nature and given the ability to think. We apply this ability in our daily lives in situations that call for any sort of cognitive activity, awareness, and consciousness. This direction allows us to analyze, to make informed decisions, to create something in the nature of a cognitive map of where we are planning to go. We are taught that when we have a problem, we should think it through; think about it, study it, analyze it; understand or discover all facets of it. In some situations, we could set up a hypothesis and envision what the outcome might be. This is the beginning of all fruitful processes and undertakings.

Nahat'á is found in the south and is associated with youth, blue evening twilight, the sacred Blue Bead or Turquoise Mountain, Tsoodzil (Mount Taylor in New

Mexico), and summer. Nahat'á is further interpreted as "planning, or to implement, to carry into full effect, to provide the means for implementation, to carry from one place to another, and to conduct in line with the mind." In the second stage or direction of the SNBH paradigm, you act upon the thoughts and decisions of the nitsáhákees stage; this involves the identification of necessary resources and all the things you will need to carry out your thinking. Here you take the initiative, gather the means of implementation, place all things in a stable way, and implement all plans. You are not doing it by yourself; you will have the help of siblings, parents, and other kin group and clan members. Everyone pitches in. Several valuable teachings originate in this direction. Elders tell us, "T'aaní anit'éégo, only you can do it." They say, "We're not going to be here to do this for you." "It's up to you." People use prayers and ceremonies in order to accomplish this stage. In doing so, they may make an offering to a small spruce tree (Frank Morgan, March 21, 1995).

West is associated with adulthood, yellow evening twilight, the sacred Abalone Shell Mountain, Dook'o'oosłííd (the San Francisco Peaks in Arizona), fall, and *iina,* interpreted as "to bring to life, to provide sustenance, to realize and make visible the outcome of thought and planning." Iina is about what the Navajo people consider life: having a family and a home, having some kind of food and a source of living (fields, farming, livestock, crafts, work), and having some kinds of ceremonials to make this complete and alive for you. It means planting your life, making it grow, making a living and accomplishing something, having a full life, and carrying forth life into the future.

This four-direction cycle concludes with the north, only to begin again with nitsáhákees in the east. North is associated with old age, folding darkness or night, the sacred Obsidian Mountain, Dibé Ntsaa (Hesperus Peak or La Plata Mountain in Colorado), winter, and *sihasin,* which means "to make strong and stable, to secure, to develop confidence, and to have a clear path." It is in the sihasin stage that you will learn whether your thinking, planning, and implementation were successful. If they were, you will want to replicate and maintain what you have accomplished, perhaps making adjustments based on your evaluation of what you have done. This is also the stage in which you will recognize the consequences of errors or neglect in your previous stages. When the cycle is repeated, you will know what to do differently to remediate the problems or errors.

In sihasin, you are progressing toward secure foundations that are necessary to make your actions or accomplishments stable, lasting, and secure. When you have repeated experiences in accomplishing worthwhile things through your own effort, motivation, and diligence, you will be settled down, having built a strong character and a positive foundation for yourself and your family. You will be secure, assured, confident, and not easily swayed by circumstances and the persuasion of others. You will have a positive self-image and the esteem of others; you will be on the path that leads to a long and happy life, and it will take you to old age.

The SNBH philosophy always leaves an opening. We are taught always to be flexible; we will always need a way out. If we don't ensure that, we will destroy ourselves. We must recognize that things that are taught as good also have a bad side. Life is not all Blessing Way; it can be harsh and we need a way to protect ourselves. We must learn to keep things in balance, but not worry about it. It is good to go out in nature and give an offering to the trees. We must have ceremonies when needed to bring ourselves back into balance and harmony, back into *hózhó*. Those are techniques that we all need.

APPLYING THE SNBH PARADIGM
TO NAVAJO LANGUAGE SHIFT

These teachings can have broad applications in anyone's life, but they have a special resonance in the lives of Navajos who are grounded in their culture. Such Navajos know that both the male/female duality and the four-stage process are predicated on the teachings of the Holy People. They are, in fact, *embodied* in the Holy People. Changing Woman, the only Navajo deity to be wholly positive and beneficent, is a good example of this embodiment. Though clearly female in gender, Changing Woman is known to have both male and female aspects. According to one account, the aspect known as Changing Woman (Asdzą́ą́ Nádleehé) is the male side of this deity, the part that is strong and assertive. The female aspect is known as White Shell Woman (Yoołgai Asdzą́ą́) after the white shells in which she was dressed her Kinaaldá ("Walked into Beauty"), or puberty ceremony. She is associated with the nurturing and loving aspects of womanhood. Through her dual nature, Changing Woman exercises both Protection Way principles and Blessing Way principles (Frank Morgan, February 14, 1995).

Changing Woman is also the deity who most strongly exemplifies and instructs us in the importance of the natural processes and cycles represented by the four seasons, the four parts of the day, the four stages of life, and the four directions. Before Changing Woman was born, the Earth Surface people were forgetting the lessons of the Holy People. They were forgetting the ways they had been taught and the relationship they were to have with the Holy People and each other. Changing Woman was born to remind them of this natural order.

After she was born on the top of Ch'ool'į́'į́ (Precious Stones, Gobernador Knob in New Mexico) and was found and taken home by Talking God (Haashch'eełti'i), only twelve days passed before she reached puberty. During this period of rapid growth and physical development for Changing Woman, the whole earth went through cycle after cycle along with her. Spring, summer, fall, and winter sped by, season following season. The times of the day—morning, noon, twilight, and night—likewise whirled by, day after day. All of earth's cycles were completed again and again. The rapid maturation of Changing Woman and the swift passage of the earth's cycles reminded people that nature was powerful and had an order, a balance, and a harmony that must be obeyed if life was to be long and happy. The lesson was that all life, all creation follows this dynamic cycle of birth, youth, maturity, and death; change and movement are normal and right. Yet this change takes place in a system that has mechanisms that restore balance and harmony and bring about all good things for those who know how to follow the path laid out by the Holy People for their children.

This is the lesson that many say Navajos of today need to be reminded of once again. "If you go out in the Navajo community or society, people are in a very negative environment now. . . . People don't operate from their home environment any more. That's supposed to be your center. If you have this, everything is in place. People have drifted away from this. Their outlook is now different. They are following outside differences. They don't have principles or orientation that goes with the hogan" (Frank Morgan, February 7, 1997).

"In order for this to work for you, you have to have a search for it," said Frank Morgan in the DEP 294 class. He continued:

It's hard to maintain a balanced path. Things happen. Your mother and father might not have raised you right. You may be on and off the perfect harmonious path. If you get too far from it, that's it; that's where it ends. You travel two paths—male Sa'ąh Naagháí and female Bik'eh Hózhóón—with balance between them. . . . Abuse and imbalance was where somebody was influenced to go off the path. People like to go off that path; they do things to upset young men and become destructive. . . . There's always negativity in any environment—kinship groups, family. When there's a student who wants to get ahead, clarify things, ask questions, there will always be those in the back who make fun, who make remarks. (February 7, 1997)

It is said that the appearance of Holy People to an elderly blind woman in remote Hard Rock Canyon in the summer of 1996 was a reminder to the Navajo people that they had been given a natural path that enables humans to pass through all the hardships and challenges and obstacles they meet. In June 1996, Albert Hale, president of the Navajo Nation, issued a memo to all tribal employees giving them leave to make a pilgrimage to the site of the visitation and suggesting that this would be the time to renew their faith and spiritual ties to their Mother Earth.

These principles of balance and process and these aspects of the spiritual path that the Holy People set forth for Navajos are equally applicable to approaching school tasks, child-raising, or building a house. And they are, I believe, more than equal to the challenge of reversing language shift.

First, one would begin in the east with nitsáhákees—thinking. In this direction, people would think about and realistically analyze the problem of Navajo language shift. They would bring to mind the state of the language today; they would recollect what they know about the language and its power and the blessings it confers; they would make decisions about what they want for the language and for themselves and their children. Their minds would begin to move in the direction of the desired outcome by assessing what linguistic and other resources they have on hand and what their limitations are. They would think and rethink the situation to be sure that what they have done will be adequate to bring about a good and lasting solution. In this way, valuable assets, including time, energy, and enthusiasm as well as finances, are not wasted in false starts and poorly conceived programs.

This is an essential stage in formulating any sort of viable strategy. It contains both Protection Way and Blessing Way elements in that it looks the threat, the danger, in the face; it assesses the terrible thing that is on the horizon—the loss of Diné Bizaad, the native language, the language of the Holy People. Furthermore, it begins to project what can be done to ward off this danger. This is the opposite of the denial of immediate danger that James Crawford (1994) has warned against and that I believe is one of the chief obstacles to a functional program of reversing Navajo language shift. Blessing Way elements would be utilized as Navajos remind themselves of what they want for themselves and work to attract what is good for them and their children.

Second, there is movement to the south and nahat'á—planning. In this direction, the careful thinking done in the previous stage is implemented in the form of plans that are based upon the thoughts and decisions. Here, people identify additional resources and the things—personnel, information, finances, and so on—that they need to carry out their plan. They determine how to secure these needed resources. This is a stage in which further teamwork is required: Who else is needed and available to assist in realizing the goal? Because there is an essential spiritual side to an undertaking, prayers and ceremonies are undertaken to complement the material features of the process.

Third, the process moves to the west, the iiná stage. This is where the thinking and planning are realized and made visible. The plan is carried out, brought to life. The program is undertaken, put into action.

The fourth and final stage is sihasin, the stage in which the fruition of the process is evaluated. Is the program effective? Is it accomplishing what was intended? Does it have a secure foundation that will allow it to continue year after year, maintaining its goal? Does it need modifications to make it more effective and satisfying?

In saying that this is a natural process, analogous to any other process in nature, I am saying that there is an order to it, that all stages in the process must be undertaken in the correct order and that all stages must be painstakingly completed. Leaving parts out and mixing up the stages can only bring unsatisfactory results and negative consequences. Plans made without careful and conscientious thought will fall through; implementation without planning will undermine confidence, alienate supporters, and create an image of incompetence and unreliability. Neglect of the evaluation of what has been put in place will allow a bright and promising start but an ignoble finish; it will result in inertia and dwindling productivity. It may give the illusion that a problem has been solved, when the reality is that a mere Band-Aid has been put on a life-threatening wound. Skipped or incomplete phases in the development and implementation of previous prescriptions and programs to halt or reverse Navajo language shift have resulted in flawed and ineffective use of personnel and financial resources.

Other problems plague Navajo language maintenance efforts. For instance, the placement of Navajo language programs in the schools has resulted in an unexpected problem. Few Navajo language supporters seem to realize that many Navajo parents and grandparents now believe that the problem of the lack of Navajo in the home has been solved and that there is nothing more to worry about. In addition, merely recommending that domains for the exclusive use of Navajo need to be protected and maintained (Slate 1993b) ignores the reality that there is unlikely to be either tribal-wide agreement on which domains to protect or individual willingness to conform to such an agreement. Too, even if there were universal agreement to perform all introductions in Navajo, this would do little to preserve or foster widespread communicative competence in the language. Finally, almost all suggestions for reversing language shift seem to imply not only that Navajos almost unanimously believe in the crucial importance of maintaining the Navajo language, but also that statements of belief about the importance of the language reflect a real willingness to *act* on that belief. One Navajo Diné College administrator told me of his belief that if the question of keeping Navajo at Diné College were put to the vote by college employees, and if people had to *do* what they voted for (that is, actually speak Navajo every day or begin to seriously study and learn the language in order to use it), then the Navajo people would vote the language down.

Though the ongoing Navajo language shift situation is very serious, it is not hopeless. A number of young people, those in their late teens and early twenties, are quite aware that many of their age group know little about their culture, have little or no fluency in the Navajo language, and are ill equipped to pass these gifts of the Holy People on to their children and their children's children. But those of this generation who do recognize this dilemma are also conscious of living at a momentous period in Navajo history. They are conscious of the role they, and others like them, can and must play in turning this situation around. Diné College student Alvina Tsosie told me, "The Navajo language is definitely in danger of dying out because less and less young people are learning to speak it. The only thing that will probably save it is the willingness of the young people to learn to speak it. Even if more parents and schools decide to teach it, it is the willingness of the young people that will make the difference." Her personal opinion, and one shared by others, is that "not knowing how to speak Navajo is not cool, knowing how to speak it is" (October 8, 1994).

Robert Jim (pseudonym), another Diné College student, demonstrated his understanding of the role he must play when he said, "As with the Diné and other tribes, prayers and ceremonies are essential with language. There is a unique language that goes with prayers and some ceremonial words are known only by the medicine man. You see, if language dies out then prayer dies out, then spirituality dies out and a beautiful people fades away. If only more individuals would not be in so much of a rut with life, then they would be able to carry on their heritage through language. It is up to us today to teach our children how to carry on their heritage and keep their language alive, as well as their people" (October 14, 1994).

Renae Walters echoed what the others had said: "And they [other young people] don't know how to talk Navajo and that's really sad. It's too bad that we're heading that way and I feel that I want to be one of the few that's not going to be that way. I want to teach my children how to talk Navajo. I want to teach them the Navajo way. I'm going to tell them about, you know, the Navajo way. I'm going to show them." She recognizes that "we're about to lose it [the Navajo language]. And we need to learn it the best way we can, so we can preserve it and so it can go on forever" (April 4, 1995).

That awareness is the key to turning the situation around. These young people must work with their elders to initiate and take charge of the revival; they must seek it and work for it. They still have access to Protection Way teachings to enable them recognize the danger and Blessing Way teachings to assist them in bringing the language into the lives of yet unborn Navajos.

ACTIVATING THE SNBH MODEL

Numerous attempts have been made to organize Navajo education according to traditional Navajo paradigms: there have been Cradleboard models, Traditional Basket models, and Corn Stalk models. A discussion of these may be read in James McNeley's article "The Pattern Which Connects Navajo and Western Knowledge" (1994). Immediately preceding the SNBH model as it has been recently been taught at Diné College was Herbert Benally's "Diné Bo'óhoo'aah Bindii'a': Navajo Philosophy of Learning," described in an article of the same name (Benally 1987). In this article, Benally provided an interpretation of Navajo traditional education as well as a Navajo framework for curriculum organization and design. According to this scheme, various types of knowledge could be placed in each of the four directions. In the east would be "all knowledge that would prepare a person to make intelligent decisions whenever he must weight values in order to determine a choice of behavior" (Benally 1987:141). The following Western categories of knowledge were placed in the east: religious studies, physical education, philosophy, ethics, aesthetics, and language.

In the south, Benally (1987:141–142) wrote, the theme was "making a living and all the knowledge and activities that go into making a living." In this direction, then, would be education, agriculture, carpentry, law, and livestock management.

The west was where "wind, thinking, planning, and gathering of family were placed. . . . The theme inherent in this direction is the social well-being of the tribe. Western studies that would correlate with these attributes are family living, sociology, history, psychology, government" (Benally 1987:142).

The north was "endowed with the black wind, rest and respectfulness" (Benally 1987:142). Academic areas involving the physical and natural sciences would be placed here; these include geology, chemistry, biology, ecology, astronomy, and physics.

The intention behind this curriculum organization, which was implemented at Navajo Community College in the late 1980s, was to balance "all four categories of Navajo knowledge so that the individual will have sound beliefs and values to make the best possible decisions, will possess skill to provide the best living for the family and provide good leadership to the family and community, and will have a sense of reverence for the earth and for all living things and for that which is in the heavens."

This four-direction framework for academic content and elements of life proved difficult for Navajos and non-Navajos alike to conceptualize, much less implement, and it was gradually phased out as a workable organizational scheme. Although some instructors and administrators (Aronilth, Morgan, and Dennison, for example) do still raise this conceptualization in their classes and other settings, for many at Diné College, the value of the SNBH paradigm in a secular educational setting is that it is being recognized as a logical and holistic process for conducting one's life—in school and out.

Therefore, when I urge the implementation of the SNBH paradigm in an effort to reverse Navajo language shift, I am not proposing that schools or school districts attempt to fit their curriculum or management objectives or even lesson plans into the four directions. Indeed, I am not proposing that this paradigm applies only to schooling.

My proposal, instead, is that Navajos look around them and think about whether their world—at the individual level, the family level, the community level, or the Navajo Nation level—would be a better, happier, more balanced and harmonious place with Navajo language and culture in it than without them. If they believe that these elements belong in their world, they might want to consider approaching the task of nurturing and encouraging the health of their Navajo language (and culture—for what is the language without the culture?) by using the SNBH process outlined here.

Reversing Navajo language shift is not the responsibility of schools, though schools can play a valuable role by providing instruction, materials, and structure. Reversing Navajo language shift is not the responsibility of the government—neither the Navajo Nation government nor the federal government—though these governments can certainly help by supporting the language through legislation and adequate funding of such legislation. Reversing Navajo language shift is not even the responsibility of the family or the community, though the power of the family and community to work together and support each other in achieving a goal can hardly be overestimated.

Whose responsibility is it, then, to reverse Navajo language shift? It is the responsibility of those persons who *need* the language in their lives and in their children's lives. Reversing Navajo language shift can be accomplished only when those individuals who *can* speak the Navajo language *do* speak it at every opportunity, when those who cannot speak the Navajo language begin taking advantage of every opportunity to *learn* to speak it, and when those who can model the benefits of speaking the Navajo language get out there and model it. It is the easiest thing in the world to tell people how to reverse Navajo language shift, but actually doing it is going to be hard. It is going to be an everyday, day after day, year after year commitment—at home, in the community, in the chapter house, at the trading post, at school, at work, at prayer, at the polls, and anywhere else a person happens to be. It is going to be hard, but it is worth doing. And it can be done.

EPILOGUE

On November 7, 2000, the voters of the state of Arizona passed Proposition 203, the "English Only Initiative," by 67 percent. The ballot read: "A 'yes' vote shall have the effect of requiring all public school instruction to be conducted in English, rather than in bilingual programs, requiring an intensive one-year English immersion program to teach English as quickly as possible while teaching academic subjects, unless parents request a waiver for those who know English, are 10 years or older or have special needs, and permitting enforcement lawsuits by parents and guardians."

This initiative was introduced by a group calling itself "English for the Children" and was put on the Arizona election ballot with the help of a $105,000 contribution from Ron Unz, a California millionaire who had engineered and seen passed a similar, but less stringent, initiative in California. The Proposition 203 document, which introduced the initiative to the Arizona voters, included an analysis by the Legislative Council, as well as a number of statements describing its pros and cons.

The Legislative Council described the fiscal impact of the proposition: "Because the Proposition would limit the amount of time that pupils could remain eligible for additional state funding for 'English Learners,' the Proposition is expected to lead to state savings. The amount of saving is difficult to predict in advance as it depends on the number of pupils who learn English quickly in the immersion classes. In addition, it is unclear how federal law would affect the transfer of students out of the immersion classes. The maximum state savings would be as high as $20.3 million in 2004 if all English learners became proficient in English within a year, although that outcome is unlikely."

Statements advocating passage of the proposition were offered by the following: English for the Children—Arizona, Ron Unz himself, Matt Salmon and John Shadegg (members of Congress), and the Valley Citizens League. They characterized the existing state bilingual education program as inflicting harm on "innocent Hispanic children" who were "trapped in segregated bilingual classrooms." They said that the only ones who supported bilingual education were the people who made money from it—educators (classroom teachers, administrators, professors) and the politicians they controlled. They asserted that the state's native Spanish-speaking students were in bilingual programs against their parents' wishes and were taught exclusively or predominantly in Spanish. Their resulting "inability to speak English dramatically limits their future earning potential and opportunities . . . to realize the American dream."

The following groups and individuals cautioned against the passage of this initiative in the "con" statements that were attached to the amendment: the Arizona Education Association, the Arizona Teachers of English Association, the Mexican American Political Association, English Plus More, Eddie Lopez, the Arizona Hispanic Community Forum, the Arizona Language Education Council, the Green Party candidates, Arizona Teachers of English to Speakers of Other Languages, the Navajo Nation Office of the President and Vice-President, Alberta Tippeconic (on behalf of the Indian tribes of Arizona), and the Arizona School Boards Association.

Many of the professional groups who opposed Proposition 203 focused on the limits it would place on the rights of parents to decide what was best for their children and the fact that under the proposition, educational decision making would become a "one-size-fits-all" matter vested solely in the state government, rather than taking place in schools and classrooms and involving trained and experienced educators and professionals. Several described this as a violation of parents' language-related civil rights. It was mentioned that the earlier English-only law, Proposition 106, which was in effect in Arizona from 1988 to 1998, had been declared unconstitutional by the Arizona Supreme Court as a violation of free speech.

Others protested that one year in an immersion English program was not enough time for the adequate acquisition of the language and that such a program would handicap and limit English learners. They cited the Arizona Department of Education's own evidence that bilingual education results in stronger English skills than English-as-a-second-language programs taught only in English.

In reference to the financial arena, these opponents of the proposition reminded voters that, in the modern world, being bilingual is a plus in global marketing and technology and that such bilingualism benefits not only the bilingual individual but also the larger population.

Educational professionals, together with Hispanic and Native American groups, added a pressing concern that was conspicuously absent from the "pro" proposition arguments—the vital role of language in the maintenance and practice of tribal traditions, religion, and culture. They correctly pointed out that the proposition targeted people of color in the state, and they characterized it as an example of racial and ethnic discrimination. Furthermore, they characterized the proposition as "mean-spirited" and "cruel and unjust." Specifically, they noted that it was a threat to Native American languages in the state because it forbade the use of children's native languages in the classroom. The Navajo Nation president and vice-president cautioned that the proposition forbade Navajo students from participating in language programs that would teach and support their Navajo language. Tippeconnic pointed out that much of tribal culture is transmitted orally, from generation to generation, by means of legends, history, stories, and values. She said: "These are living languages, used daily by Indian people in their homes, in business, and in public and governmental affairs." Use of English *and* the native language is important in all these settings. She concluded that Proposition 203 was an "attempt to destroy Indian culture and the freedoms on which this country was founded."

In addition to reading these statements, I read all the issues of the Navajo tribal newspaper, the *Navajo Times,* from July 2000 (when the possibility of the initiative's appearing on the fall ballot was first mentioned) through February 2001 (the time when I wrote this epilogue). As I read dozens of arguments by tribal officials, educators, parents, and Navajo citizens, and as I spoke with Navajo friends and colleagues, something struck me: namely, how completely most of these people appeared to have bought into the argument that schools are the last, best hope for the perpetuation of the Navajo language. Their discourse tends to support the thesis I have argued in this book—that a vast number of Navajos believe not only that schools can and should teach the Navajo language but also that teaching and using Navajo in the schools will result in the continued life of this language.

I personally agree with those who opposed Proposition 203. I concur that it is a mean-spirited and unjust invasion of the rights and freedoms of the students, their parents, and educators. I agree that this and similar propositions are far from being in the best interests of the affected students and communities. It goes against everything that linguists and educators know about acquisition of a second language. It is at best an ignorant and at worst a hateful piece of interference in the lives of American citizens. I strongly agree that it strikes a blow against the teaching and maintenance of students' home languages. I agree that it is racist, and I would add that it is classist. It appears to me that the monied white citizens of Arizona are thinking of their own pocketbooks and, despite their protestations to the contrary, their need for an undereducated class of workers. What I do not agree with is that the entire future of native languages can and should be thought of as resting in the law-making hands of the voters of Arizona.

Think for a minute about why these languages are important, what they are needed for. Over and over I hear that they are needed for communication within the tribal population and within families; they are needed in ceremonies and for prayer and singing; they are needed for the transmission of cultural wisdom from generation to generation. They are also needed in the schools so that English learners can more thoroughly learn the English language and the core content of Western schooling.

Therefore, while it is certainly the most desirable and just thing to do, and it is something that Arizona voters should continue to work toward, the teaching and use of native languages in the schools is not the only or the most important way to support these languages. It is very positive and important to have these language programs, but they should be thought of as supplemental to what goes on in the world outside of school.

When I was growing up in rural Arkansas, we had a saying about its being unwise to put all your eggs in one basket. That is what I am cautioning against here. It is dangerous to count on federal or state governments to consistently have native people's best interests at heart. These are, after all, the very governments that historically did their best to eradicate native peoples, their languages, and their cultures through policies that ranged from genocidal to merely assimilationist. When they have supported Indian interests from time to time—through legislation such as the Native American Language Act, for instance—they have not made adequate funding available for meaningful implementation. It is short-sighted to expect that they will adequately protect and foster the sacred and cultural traditions that are the heart of Navajo or other native culture. Governments can and should have an important part to play, but they cannot and will not do it with the commitment and conviction that is needed.

Again, my suggestion is that the contexts in which the Navajo language is used, is needed, or is required are the contexts in which the bulk of it should be taught and nurtured. Schools and the governments that control them can and should supplement and complement and support the use of the language, but they cannot carry the entire responsibility. Laws and lawmakers are too ephemeral, too variable to carry such a precious responsibility. As I write, twenty-three states have passed measures similar to Proposition 203; three states neighboring Arizona—Utah, Colorado, and New Mexico—have passed or are targeted to introduce similar legislation. The group U.S. English is gearing up for another assault at the national level.

My suggestion to Navajos and other Native Americans, then, is to keep on playing a role in government, keep on working with and enlisting the support of linguists, anthropologists, and educators. Keep on teaching us how we can assist and support you. Keep on working to get the ear of the wider American public, to educate them about Indian priorities. Keep on working to get out the vote—Navajo and other Native American voters, but also the vote of the rest of the county, state, or national population who believe in fairness and justice and who are eager to do the right thing, once they know and understand what it is.

Legislation, favorable policies, and adequate funding come and go; families, communities, and dedicated individuals persist. Navajos have gone through some of the most difficult experiences human beings can endure and survive. They must recognize this time for what it is—a historical watershed in which the future of the Navajo language will be decided. It is an opportunity to fight, to be warriors for the language, for the culture, for the persistence of Navajos as a distinct people for millennia to come.

REFERENCES

ABU-LUGHOD, LILA 1991 Writing against Culture. *In* Recapturing Anthropology: Working in the Present. Richard G. Fox, ed. Pp. 137–162. Santa Fe: School of American Research Press.

ACREY, BILL P. 1979 Navajo History: The Land and the People. Shiprock, NM: Department of Curriculum Materials Development, Central Consolidated School District No. 22.

ADAMS, DAVID WALLACE 1995 Education for Extinction: American Indians and the Boarding School Experience 1875–1928. Lawrence: University of Kansas Press.

ANZALDÚA, GLORIA 1987 Borderlands/La Frontera: The New Mestiza. San Francisco: Spinsters/Aunt Lute.

ARONILTH, WILSON, JR. n.d. Foundation of Navajo Culture. Unpublished MS.

BAHR, DONALD 1989 Indians and Missions: Homage to the Debate with Rupert Costo and Jeannette Henry. Journal of the Southwest 31:300–329.

BECENTI, DEENISE 1997 Non-Indian Draws Reaction on Ye'ii Bicheii. Navajo Times, May 1, A-9.

BENALLY, ANCITA, AND T. L. McCARTY 1990 The Navajo Language Today. *In* Perspectives on Official English: The Campaign for English as the Official Language of the USA. Karen L. Adams and Daniel T. Brink, eds. Pp. 237–245. Berlin: Mouton de Gruyter.

BENALLY, HERBERT 1987 Diné Bó'hoo'aah Bindii'á: Navajo Philosophy of Learning. Diné Be'iina 1(1):113–148.

BINGHAM, SAM, AND JANET BINGHAM, EDS. 1982 Between Sacred Mountains: Navajo Stories and Lessons from the Land. Chinle, AZ: Rock Point Community School Press.

BLATCHFORD, PAUL 1977 Paul Blatchford. *In* Stories of Traditional Life and Culture: Ałk'idą́ą́'yę́ę̨k'ehgo Diné Kéé'dahat'íńę̨ę̨ Baa Nahane' by Twenty-two Navajo Men and Women. Broderick H. Johnson, ed. Pp. 173–181, Tsaile, AZ: Navajo Community College Press.

BRANDT, ELIZABETH 1988 Applied Linguistic Anthropology and American Indian Language Renewal. Human Organization 47(4):322–329.

CHOW, REY 1994 Where Have All the Natives Gone? In Displacements: Cultural Identities in Question. Angelika Bammer, ed. Pp. 125–151. Bloomington: University of Indiana Press.

CLIFTON, JAMES A., ED. 1989 Being and Becoming Indian: Biographical Studies of North American Frontiers. Chicago: Dorsey Press.

COOMBS, L. MADISON 1962 Doorway toward the Light: The Story of the Special Navajo Education Program. Washington, DC: United States Department of the Interior, Bureau of Indian Affairs, Branch of Education.

CRAWFORD, JAMES 1994 Endangered Native American Languages: What Is to Be Done, and Why? Journal of Navajo Education 11(3):3–11.

DENETSOSIE, HOKE 1977 Hoke Denetsosie. In Stories of Traditional Life and Culture: Ałk'idą́ą́'yę́ę́k'ehgo Diné Kéé'dahat'íńę́ę́ Baa Nahane' by Twenty-two Navajo Men and Women. Broderick H. Johnson, ed. Pp. 73–104. Tsaile, AZ: Navajo Community College Press.

DEYHLE, DONNA 1983 Between Games and Failure: A Micro-Ethnographic Study of Navajo Students and Testing. Curriculum Inquiry 13(4):347–376.

1986a Break Dancing and Breaking Out: Anglos, Utes, and Navajos in a Border Reservation High School. Anthropology and Education Quarterly 17:111–127.

1986b Success and Failure: A Micro-Ethnographic Comparison of Navajo and Anglo Students' Perceptions of Testing. Curriculum Inquiry 16(4):365–389.

1995 Navajo Youth and Anglo Racism: Cultural Integrity and Resistance. Harvard Educational Review 65(3):403–444.

DICK, JOHN 1977 John Dick. In Stories of Traditional Life and Culture: Ałk'idą́ą́"'yę́ę́k'ehgo Diné Kéé'dahat'íńę́ę́ Baa Nahane' by Twenty-Two Navajo Men and Women. Broderick H. Johnson, ed. Pp. 182–200. Tsaile, AZ: Navajo Community College Press.

DINÉ COLLEGE 1997 General Catalog 1997–1998. Tsaile, AZ: Diné College.

DONOVAN, BILL 1997 Reservation Unemployment Up to 45 Percent. Navajo Times, May 8:A-1, A-3.

EMERSON, GLORIA J. 1983 Navajo Education. In Handbook of North American Indians, vol. 10, Southwest. Alfonso Ortiz, ed. Pp. 659–678. Washington, DC: Smithsonian Institution.

FARELLA, JOHN R. 1984 The Main Stalk: A Synthesis of Navajo Philosophy. Tucson: The University of Arizona Press.

FISHMAN, JOSHUA 1991 Reversing Language Shift. Clevedon, England: Multilingual Matters.

1996   What Do You Lose When You Lose Your Language? *In* Stabilizing Indigenous Languages. Gina Cantoni, ed. Pp. 80–91. Flagstaff, AZ: Northern Arizona University, Center for Excellence in Education.

FRANCIS, SANDRA T.   1997   Confab Is Start of Understanding. (Letter to the editor.) Navajo Times, May 1, A-4.

FUCHS, ESTELLE, AND ROBERT J. HAVIGHURST   1972   To Live on This Earth: American Indian Education. Garden City, NJ: Anchor Press/Doubleday.

GOFFMAN, ERVING   1963   Stigma: Notes on the Management of Spoiled Identity. Englewood Cliffs, NJ: Prentice Hall.

GRAMSCI, ANTONIO   1971   Selections from the Prison Notebooks of Antonio Gramsci. New York: International Press.

HALE, KENNETH, WITH COLLETTE CRAIG, NORA ENGLAND, LAVERNE MASAYESVA JEANNE, MICHAEL KRAUSS, LUCILLE WATAHOMIGIE, AND AKIRA YAMAMOTO
1992   Language Endangerment and the Human Value of Linguistic Diversity. Language 68(1):1–42

HANLEY, MAX 1977 Max Hanley. *In* Stories of Traditional Life and Culture: Ałk'idą́ą́'yę́ęk'ehgo Diné Kéé'dahat'íńę́ę Baa Nahane' by Twenty-two Navajo Men and Women. Broderick H. Johnson, ed. Pp. 17–55. Tsaile, AZ: Navajo Community College Press.

HENZE, ROSEMARY C., AND LAUREN VANETT   1993   To Walk in Two Worlds—Or More? Challenging a Common Metaphor of Native Education. Anthropology and Education Quarterly 24(2):116–134.

HOLM, WAYNE   1971   Bilagáana Bizaad: ESL/EFL in a Navajo Bilingual Setting. Paper delivered at the TESOL Conference, New Orleans, March 6.

1993   On the Use of Navajo Language in Navajo Head Start Centers: Preliminary Considerations. Journal of Navajo Education 10(3):36–45.

HOLM, WAYNE, AND AGNES HOLM   1990   Rock Point, a Navajo Way to Go to School: A Valediction. Annals of the American Academy of Political and Social Sciences 508:170–184.

HOOKS, BELL   1995   Killing Rage: Ending Racism. New York: Henry Holt.

HOUSE, DEBORAH, AND JON REYHNER   1996   Adult Education Session. *In* Stabilizing Indigenous Languages. Gina Cantoni, ed. Pp. 143–149. Flagstaff, AZ: Northern Arizona University, Center for Excellence in Education.

IVERSON, PETER   1981   The Navajo Nation. Albuquerque: University of New Mexico Press.

1983   The Emerging Navajo Nation. *In* Handbook of North American Indians, vol. 10, Southwest. Alfonso Ortiz, ed. Pp. 636–640. Washington, DC: Smithsonian Institution.

JOHN, VERA P.   1972   Styles of Learning—Styles of Teaching: Reflections on the Education of Navajo Children. *In* Functions of Language in the Classroom. Courtney B. Cazden, Vera P. John, and Dell Hymes, eds. Pp. 331–343. New York: Teachers College Press.

KRAUSS, MICHAEL   1996   Status of Native American Language Endangerment. *In* Stabilizing Indigenous Languages. Gina Cantoni, ed. Pp. 16–21. Flagstaff, AZ: Northern Arizona University, Center for Excellence in Education.

KRUPAT, ARNOLD   1992   Ethnocriticism: Ethnography, History, Literature. Berkeley: University of California Press.

LINK, MARTIN A.   1968   Navajo: A Century of Progress, 1868–1968. Window Rock, AZ: The Navajo Tribe and K. D. Publications.

LOMAWAIMA, K. TSIANINA   1994   They Called It Prairie Light: The Story of Chilocco Indian School. Lincoln: University of Nebraska Press.

MACIONIS, JOHN J.   1998   Society: The Basics. Englewood Cliffs, NJ: Prentice Hall.

MCBETH, SALLY J.   1983   Ethnic Identity and the Boarding School Experience of West-Central Oklahoma American Indians. New York: University Press of America.

MCCARTY, T. L.   1989   School as Community: The Rough Rock Demonstration. Harvard Educational Review 59(4):484–503.

1996   Schooling, Resistance, and American Indian Languages. Paper presented at the annual meeting of the American Anthropological Association, San Francisco, CA, November 21, 1996.

MCCARTY, T. L., REGINA HADLEY LYNCH, STEPHEN WALLACE, AND ANCITA BENALLY
1991   Classroom Inquiry and Navajo Learning Styles: A Call for Reassessment. Anthropology and Education Quarterly 22:42–59.

MCLAUGHLIN, DANIEL   1990   The Sociolinguistics of Navajo Literacy. Journal of Navajo Education 7(2):28–36.

1992   When Literacy Empowers: Navajo Language in Print. Albuquerque: University of New Mexico Press.

MCNELEY, JAMES K.   1981   Holy Wind in Navajo Philosophy. Tucson: University of Arizona Press.

1994   The Pattern Which Connects Navajo and Western Knowledge. Journal of Navajo Education 12(1):3–14.

MERIAM, LEWIS, ED.   1928   The Problem of Indian Administration. Baltimore, MD: Johns Hopkins University Press.

MERTZ, ELIZABETH   1992   Linguistic Ideology and Praxis in U.S. Law School Classrooms. Pragmatics 2(3):325–334.

NAVAJO NATION CENSUS   1993   1990 Census: Population and Housing Characteristics of the Navajo Nation. Window Rock, AZ: Navajo Nation, Division of Community Development.

ORTIZ, SIMON   1993   The Language We Know. *In* Growing Up Native American. Patricia Riley, ed. Pp. 29–38. New York: Avon.

PARMAN, DONALD L.   1972   J. C. Morgan, Navajo Apostle of Assimilation. Prologue (Journal of the National Archives), Summer, pp. 83–98.

PARSONS-YAZZIE, EVANGELINE   1995   Navajo-Speaking Parents' Perceptions of Reasons for Navajo Language Attrition. Journal of Navajo Education 13(1):29–38.

PFEIFFER, ANITA   1996   Standing on the Shoulders of Others: Diné Teacher Education in Historical Perspective. Presentation at Navajo Community College, Tsaile, AZ, September 13.

PHILIPS, SUSAN U.   1998   Language Ideologies in Institutions of Power: A Commentary. In Language Ideologies: Practice and Theory. Bambi B. Schieffelin, Paul V. Kroskrity, and Kathryn A. Woolard, eds. Pp. 211–228. New York: Oxford University Press.

PLATERO, PAUL R.   1992a   Language Loss among Navajo Children. Paper presented at the Athabaskan Linguistics Conference, Flagstaff, AZ, July 4.

  1992b   Navajo Head Start Language Study. Abridged version. Window Rock, AZ: Navajo Division of Education.

PRUCHA, FRANCIS PAUL   1975   Documents of United States Indian Policy. Lincoln: University of Nebraska Press.

QOYAWAYMA, POLINGAYSI (ELIZABETH Q. WHITE), AS TOLD TO VADA F. CARLSON
  1964   No Turning Back: A Hopi Woman's Struggle to Live in Two Worlds. Albuquerque: University of New Mexico Press.

REICHARD, GLADYS A.   1944   Prayer: The Compulsive Word. American Ethnological Society Monograph 7. Seattle: University of Washington Press.

  1950   Navaho Religion: A Study of Symbolism. New York: Bollingen Foundation/Pantheon Books.

REYHNER, JON   1992   Emphasizing the Positive Aspects of the Culture. In Teaching the Native American. Hap Gilliland, ed. Pp. 27–39. Dubuque, IA: Kendall/Hunt Publishing Company.

ROESSEL, ROBERT A., JR.   1979   Navajo Education, 1948–1978: Its Progress and Its Problems. Rough Rock, AZ: Navajo Curriculum Center, Rough Rock Demonstration School.

ROESSEL, RUTH, ED.   1971   Navajo Studies at Navajo Community College. Many Farms, AZ: Navajo Community College Press.

ROSIER, PAUL, AND WAYNE HOLM   1980   The Rock Point Experience: A Longitudinal Study of a Navajo School. Washington, DC: Center for Applied Linguistics.

SAID, EDWARD   1993   Culture and Imperialism. New York: Vintage Books.

SANCHEZ, GEORGE   1948   The People: A Study of the Navajos. Washington, DC: United States Indian Service.

SARRIS, GREG   1993   Keeping Slug Woman Alive: A Holistic Approach to American Indian Texts. Berkeley: University of California Press.

SEKAQUAPTEWA, HELEN (AS TOLD TO LOUISE UDALL)   1969   Me and Mine: The Life Story of Helen Sekaquaptewa. Tucson: University of Arizona Press.

SHAW, ANNA MOORE   1974   A Pima Past. Tucson: University of Arizona Press.

SHONERD, HENRY G.   1990   Domesticating the Barbarous Tongue: Language Policy for the Navajo in Historical Perspective. Language Problems and Language Planning 14(3):193–208.

SLATE, CLAY   1993a   On Reversing Navajo Language Shift. Journal of Navajo Education 10(3):30–35.

   1993b   Finding a Place for Navajo. Tribal College, Spring, pp. 10–14.

SPOLSKY, BERNARD   1975a   Prospects for the Survival of the Navajo Language. *In* Linguistics and Anthropology, in Honor of C. F. Voegelin. M. Dale Kinkade, Kenneth Hale, and Oswald Werner, eds. Pp. 597–606. Lisse, Netherlands: Peter de Ridder Press.

   1975b   Linguistics in Practice: The Navajo Reading Study Program. Theory into Practice 15:347–352.

STEWART, IRENE   1980   A Voice in Her Tribe: A Navajo Woman's Own Story. Doris Ostrander Dawdy, ed. Socorro, NM: Ballena Press.

SZASZ, MARGARET   1974   Education and the American Indian: The Road to Self-Determination since 1928. Albuquerque: University of New Mexico Press.

TAUSSIG, MICHAEL   1993   Mimesis and Alterity: A Particular History of the Senses. New York: Routledge Press.

THOMPSON, HILDEGARD   1975   The Navajos' Long Walk for Education: A History of Navajo Education. Tsaile, AZ: Navajo Community College Press.

TRENNERT, ROBERT A., JR.   1988   The Phoenix Indian School: Forced Assimilation in Arizona, 1891–1935. Norman: University of Oklahoma Press.

U.S. SENATE   1969   Indian Education: A National Tragedy—A National Challenge. Report of the Committee on Labor and Public Welfare, Special Subcommittee on Indian Education, 91st Cong., 1st sess. Washington, DC: U.S. Government Printing Office.

VELTMAN, CALVIN   1983   Language Shift in the United States. Berlin: Mouton.

WILLIAMS, RAYMOND   1977   Marxism and Literature. Oxford: Oxford University Press.

WITHERSPOON, GARY   1971   Navajo Categories of Objects at Rest. American Anthropologist 73:110–127.

   1974   The Central Concepts of Navajo World View (I). Linguistics 119 (January):41–59.

   1975   The Central Concepts of Navajo World View (II). Linguistics 161:69–88.

   1977   Language and Art in the Navajo Universe. Ann Arbor: University of Michigan Press.

1983 Language and Reality in Navajo World View. *In* Handbook of North American Indians, vol. 10, Southwest. Alfonso Ortiz, ed. Pp. 570–578. Washington, DC: Smithsonian Institution.

YAVA, ALBERT 1978 Big Falling Snow: A Tewa-Hopi Indian's Life and Times and the History and Traditions of His People. Harold Courlander, ed. Albuquerque: University of New Mexico Press.

YAZZIE, EVANGELINE 1995 A Study of Reasons for Navajo Language Attrition as Perceived by Navajo Speaking Parents. Ph.D. diss., Northern Arizona University, Flagstaff, AZ.

YOUNG, ROBERT W. 1983 Apachean Languages. *In* Handbook of North American Indians, vol. 10, Southwest. Alfonso Ortiz, ed. Pp. 393–400. Washington, DC: Smithsonian Institution.

1993 The Evolution of Written Navajo: An Historical Sketch. Journal of Navajo Education 10(3):46–55.

ZEPEDA, OFELIA, AND JANE H. HILL 1991 The Conditions of Native American Languages in the United States. *In* Endangered Languages. Robert H. Robins and Eugenius M. Uhlenbeck, eds. Pp. 135–155. New York: Berg Press.

INDEX

traditionalism, 13, 14

Treaty of 1868, 4, 8; terms of peace, 57

Tsaile (Ariz.), xi, xv, xvi

tsiiyééł, 79

"us-them" dichotomy, 38. *See also* oppositional dichotomy

victimist history, 39

victimist identity, 39–40. *See also* Long Walk;
boarding schools

Vocational Rehabilitation Bill, 11

Walters, Harry, 48, 60, 92

Walters, Renae, xxii–xxiii, 41, 64–65, 101

Western education, 4–6

westernization, 65

Williams, Raymond, 13

Witherspoon, Gary, xxi, xxiii–xxiv

World War II, 7, 15

Young, Robert, 7

ABOUT THE AUTHOR

Deborah House has master's degrees in anthropology and in teaching English as a second language, and a doctorate in linguistic anthropology. She is an assistant professor in the Department of Sociology, Anthropology, and Social Work at Texas Tech University in Lubbock. Her current research interests include Navajo language shift and the role of Navajo language proficiency in the maintenance of an "authentic" Navajo identity; Ozark mountain identity; and contemporary Navajo conceptions of women's public roles.